"An original and entertaining introduction to economics. This delightful collection of stories from around the world illustrates complex ideas in a simple and appealing way which can be enjoyed by readers of all ages."
Enrico Spolaore, Professor of Economics, Tufts University (USA)

"A uniquely valuable contribution to our children's literature that deserves to be widely read."
Glenn C. Loury, Professor of Economics, Brown University (USA)

"A fantastic ride through a mosaic of geography, culture and economics...a profound conversation with people all over the world in their own languages...a cheerful insight into our universal brotherhood."
Matthias Cinyabuguma, Senior Economist, World Bank

"A gentle introduction to economics for kids. Recommended."
Ivo Welch, Professor of Finance, UCLA Anderson School of Management (USA)

"A simple yet thorough journey through economics 101. I have no doubt this will be a major asset in the hands of history, business and economics teachers and students."
Stephen Lowry, Principal, Waterford Kamhlaba- United World College of Southern Africa (Swaziland)

"A wonderful introduction to the key principles of economics through storytelling."
Patrick Awuah, Founder and President, Ashesi University (Ghana)

"A most original book...which provides so much food for thought."
Anna Aizer, Associate Professor of Economics, Brown University (USA)

Economics through Everyday Stories from around the World

Elena Fernandez Prados

First Published in 2016

Copyright © 2016 Elena Fernandez Prados
All rights reserved.

All characters and events in this publication, other than those clearly in the public domain, are fictitious and any resemblance to real persons, living or dead, is purely coincidental.

No part of this publication may be reproduced, stored in a retrieval system, or transmitted, in any form or by any means, without the prior permission in writing of the author.

A CIP catalogue record for this book is available from the British Library.

ISBN: 978-1523296415

To my daughter, Maria

Contents

1. **THE ECONOMY:** THE CAPE VERDEAN GIRL AND HER GRANDMOTHER 1

2. **ECONOMIC CYCLES:** THE JAMAICAN HOTEL MAID 5

3. **PRODUCTIVITY:** THE AFGHAN PISTACHIO FARMER 9

4. **DEMAND AND SUPPLY:** THE COLOMBIAN *HACIENDA* OWNER 12

5. **PRICE-SETTING MECHANISM:** THE PAKISTANI BUSINESSMAN 16

6. **RESPONSE TO PRICE CHANGES:** THE JAPANESE RETIRED ACCOUNTANT 19

7. **PURCHASING POWER:** THE GHANAIAN COCOA FARMER 22

8. **COMPETITION AND LIVING STANDARDS:** THE MOROCCAN SOFTWARE ENGINEER 27

9. **INTERNATIONAL TRADE:** THE SPANISH CARPENTER 31

10. **INFLATION:** THE ARGENTINIAN STUDENT 35

11. **FOREIGN EXCHANGE:** THE KENYAN MARKETING DIRECTOR 39

12. **JOB CREATION:** THE GREEK NEWS PRESENTER 43

13. **THE ROLE OF GOVERNMENT IN THE ECONOMY:** THE CONGOLESE MAYOR 47

14. **RISK AND RETURN:** THE ITALIAN ANTHROPOLOGIST 51

15. **SAVINGS AND INVESTMENTS:** THE SRI LANKAN NURSERY OWNER 55

16. **FINANCIAL ACCOUNTING:** THE IRANIAN APPRENTICE BAKER 60

17. **CIVIC VALUES:** THE CUBAN SALSA DANCER 63

FOREWORD BY THE AUTHOR

Some readers may call this a children's book: they are right. This book is for children aged nine to ninety! It is for anyone who wants to unravel the mysteries of economics with the clarity and simplicity of reading tales.

From the tranquil settings of a Ghanaian village to the bustling alleys of an Iranian bazaar, this collection of stories will take you through a journey around the globe, meeting new characters who speak different languages and have different cultures but who all experience the reality of economics in their daily lives.

1. THE ECONOMY: THE CAPE VERDEAN GIRL AND HER GRANDMOTHER

Amalia Evora is an eight-year-old girl from Praia, the capital city of Cape Verde. Cape Verde is an archipelago of islands scattered across the Atlantic Ocean, hundreds of kilometers off the coast of West Africa.

Like many girls of her age, Amalia likes going to the cinema, reading adventure books, and swimming in the sea, but above all, Amalia loves eating yogurts. Amalia lives in a cozy, two-story house with a garden overlooking the island of Santa Maria. She shares her house with her little brother, her parents, and her grandma, Cesaria. Amalia loves her grandma because she tells her fantastic stories from the past and teaches her how to sing beautiful and poignant folk songs called *mornas*.

One day, Amalia returns home from school. She opens the gate of the house and finds Grandma sitting under the almond tree. She is looking very sad. In fact, she is crying! Amalia runs toward Grandma and asks her what is wrong. "Is something hurting you?"

Grandma shows her a very old black-and-white photograph that she is holding in between her wrinkled hands. "Look, Amalia, this was me years ago, when I was your age, and this is my sister, Heloisa." Amalia looks at the photograph closely, but she can barely recognize the people on it. All she can see are two very skinny-looking girls with big black eyes popping out of their faces and very sad expressions. "Grandma," she asks, "why do you look so worried in the picture? Were you having a bad day when it was taken?"

Grandma grabs Amalia's little hand and asks her to take a seat next to her under the almond tree. "Yes, my darling," she says, "I was having a bad day on the morning the photographer took that picture. In fact, times were really hard for us when I was a child growing up in Cape Verde.

Back then, the island's economy was closed, and we relied primarily on farming and fishing for employment and income. Both activities were equally backbreaking but generated very little income.

As farmers, my parents—your great-grandparents—really struggled to put enough food on the table for all of us. We cultivated onions, corn, and sweet potatoes, but you know that the weather in Cape Verde is very dry all year long. It does not rain much, and we often went through periods of drought when all our crops dried out and there was very little for us to eat."

"Hmm," interrupts Amalia, "I am feeling very hungry now." And so she runs to the kitchen, grabs a yogurt, and returns to the garden to continue listening to Grandma's story while she devours her food.

"The other major economic activity in Cape Verde, back in those days, was fishing. A lot of men, like my cousin Rafael, were fishermen. They built small wooden canoes, weaved fishing nets, and went into the sea to catch tuna. But fishing was a very dangerous business. The ocean can get very rough on stormy days, and unfortunately some of our men left Praia in a canoe and never returned! We sang *mornas* to remember those who never came back. Those who returned were grateful: they had risked their lives for a few tuna fish! That was the cost of a man's life back then," Grandma says.

"And what about school, Grandma? How was your school back then? Did it look like the one I go to?" interrupts Amalia.

"My darling," Grandma replies, "back then there were no schools on the island. Children were expected to work on the fields or in the sea with their parents. We were illiterate. We never learned how to read or write, and we could count only using our fingers."

"Back then our country was very poor," Grandma continues. "Many of my cousins emigrated to the United States and Portugal to find a better life. Over there, they took up jobs as farm laborers, domestic servants, and even whale hunters! When they left, we cried a lot, and we sang *mornas*, for we knew that we may never see them again. Back in the day, traveling abroad by boat was very expensive, and the journey could take several weeks!

Because the economy of Cape Verde was closed for the most part," Grandma explains, "we were limited to the little that was produced on the island. However, once a year, a vessel from Lisbon would stop by the port of Praia, and people would trade agricultural produce for very fine European clothes and metal cutlery that we cherished fondly. Actually, those items were so precious to us that we barely used them. We stored them safely in our closets and only used them on very special occasions.

Overtime, technological advances made the cost of transporting goods from one country to another much cheaper. The vessel from Lisbon now stopped three times a year, and the fine clothes and cutlery from Europe started to become more affordable. All of a sudden, we could buy and sell more goods, and we started owning things that made our lives a little easier.

Cheaper transportation also meant that our cousins from Portugal and the United States could visit us more often. Whenever they visited, they brought new ideas and money to help us set up businesses on the island. My cousin Rafael, for example, brought home from Lisbon 20,000 escudos, which was a fortune at the time. With that money he built a big fishing boat for his siblings so that they could catch more fish and be much safer in the sea on those stormy days when canoes were easily tossed around by strong winds.

Gradually the economy started growing and diversifying. More people found jobs outside of agriculture and fishing, and we all started to eat much better! In one of his trips back home, my cousin Rafael brought a machine that was able to drill the ground and make a borehole. This helped us set up an irrigation system that kept our crops watered all year long. We were no longer solely reliant on rain water. Thanks to the wonders of technological innovation!

Overtime, tourism started becoming popular on the island, and new hotels and restaurants were established creating many new jobs. With rising income levels, many banks, telecom companies, retail outlets, and construction companies opened up on the island. As the economy expanded, the government of Cape Verde was able to collect more tax revenue and use those funds to build schools for children and hospitals for sick people. It also built several new roads and even an airport in Praia! As life got better, many of our cousins who had emigrated abroad returned home. It was a real joy to see our people come back to their homeland!

Life has gotten much better for everyone in Cape Verde," Grandma explains. "Our quality of life has improved a lot, and we now have access to so many more things. Back in the day, there were no cars around, just donkeys. There was no Internet, no swimming pools, and certainly no yogurts. So you should not take everything you have for granted, my little one!"

"Now that you have mentioned it," Amalia says, "I really feel like having another yogurt. Your stories always make me hungry, Grandma."

Key Concepts:

- The economy refers to the way a country allocates its resources (such as workers, natural resources, and capital) in order to produce goods and services.

- The size of an economy (its gross domestic product, or GDP) refers to the total value of goods and services produced by all workers in a country over a given period of time.

- The wealth of a country's citizens can be assessed by comparing the total value of economic output with the size of its population (GDP per person). Countries with higher GDP per person enjoy higher income levels and generally better living standards.

- Living standards improve as workers become more productive and are able to produce goods and services of higher economic value.

- GDP per person is a useful indicator of living standards in a country, but it is not a perfect measure of all the activities that create value for people. GDP does not capture the value of intangible goods, such as friendship, family relationships, and social support networks.

2. ECONOMIC CYCLES: THE JAMAICAN HOTEL MAID

Jamaica is a beautiful island in the Caribbean Sea. Its economy is heavily reliant on tourism for income and employment. The majority of tourists to Jamaica are American families that want to enjoy the island's sandy beaches and invigorating sunshine.

Latoya Brown is a twenty-eight-year-old lady from Port Antonio, a small coastal town in eastern Jamaica. She lives in a city-center apartment with her husband, Ray, and their twelve-year-old son, Tyrone. Both Latoya and Ray work in the tourism industry. Latoya is a housekeeper at a five-star resort very popular with American visitors, while Ray grills spicy fish on the beach and sells them to hungry tourists eager to taste Jamaican delicacies.

Latoya has been working at the beach resort for the past three years, and she enjoys her routine. She gets to work at seven o'clock in the morning, changes into her uniform, and starts servicing rooms. She first changes the bed linen, making sure there are no creases on it. Then she tidies up the room, mops the bathroom floor, and replaces the guest's towels with clean ones. Sometimes she decorates the rooms with fragrant red flowers. Other times she applies herself to creating interesting shapes using bathroom towels that she then places carefully on the bed to the delight of tourists. This can sometimes be time-consuming, but she works at a luxury resort after all, where hotel maids are expected to do much more than just cleaning and tidying up.

Latoya likes her job, although it can get a bit lonely sometimes. Hotel maids are expected to be discreet, almost invisible, and Latoya finds that boring. That is why she has devised some little games to keep her mind busy while she is servicing rooms. When she enters a new room, Latoya likes to guess what type of guest is staying in it: man or woman, young or old? What could their profession be? And what could be bringing them to Jamaica: a heartbreak, a promotion, the desire to explore new places?

Latoya walks around the room just like a detective would, looking for any clues that could lead to a probable answer. And clues come in various shapes and forms—sometimes in the form of a lipstick, sometimes in the form of an antiwrinkle cream, and sometimes simply in the form of a good old pair of black shoes. Over the years, Latoya has gotten so good at the guessing game that she can just walk into a room and describe the person who is staying in it with a high degree of certainty.

One day, just like any other day, Latoya reports to work at seven o'clock in the morning, but before she even has time to change into her uniform, the manager calls her and her colleagues into a large meeting room. Latoya instantly senses that nothing good can come out of this. She is right.

The hotel manager goes on and on talking about something to do with a financial crisis in the United States, a decline in tourist arrivals to Jamaica, and a loss in the income statement of...God knows what. Finally, the bomb drops: a large number of housekeeping staff are to be fired, including herself—Latoya Brown.

Latoya runs home in tears and shares the bad news with her husband. "Almighty Lord!" Ray cries, "it is too bad that you have lost your job because I am also struggling. For the past few months, I have noticed that there are fewer tourists on the beach, and I am not able to sell as much grilled fish as before. *This is no good*, darling. But don't you worry. Why don't you try to get some cleaning job at some rich folk's home, while I will take on a night job playing the guitar at Marley's Beach Bar? This should help us get by."

Latoya is slightly relieved, but she soon realizes that without her monthly salary, she will have to make some sacrifices. Before she got fired, Latoya always had some money to spare at the end of the month. She liked going to the salon every month to change her hairstyle and get a manicure. Now she will have to forgo those little luxuries, and instead do her hair and nails at home in order to save money.

A few days later, Tyrone, Latoya's twelve-year-old son, returns home from school with bad news. "Mom," Tyrone says, "there have been some changes in my school that I am not happy about. Lunch is no longer free, and we now have to pay for our books, pencils, and notebooks."

"Why is that?" asks Latoya very surprised.

"I don't know, Mom," Tyrone replies. "Our principal went on about some financial crisis in the United States, a drop in tourist arrivals to Jamaica, and a decline in government tax receipts, and somehow that has something to do with our school's budget being under pressure," he explains. Latoya does not really understand what all this means, but she knows her family is in deep trouble.

The following Sunday, Latoya, Ray, and Tyrone attend their local Pentecostal church as they usually do. At church, Latoya gets introduced to Mrs. Millington, an expatriate American woman living in Jamaica. Mrs. Millington is well known to everyone: she is the wife of a wealthy hotel manager, and she lives in Montego Bay, one of the most exclusive residential areas on the island. Latoya remembers Ray's suggestion and timidly asks Mrs. Millington whether she needs any help cleaning her house. To her big surprise, Mrs. Millington replies that she is indeed looking for a house help and that she would like to engage her services as soon as possible.

The following morning, Ray drives Latoya to Montego Bay on the motorbike that he purchased with the money he managed to save over the years selling grilled fish to tourists. As they enter the residential area where Mrs. Millington lives, Latoya tells her husband, "Check out these mansions, darling. I dream that one day Tyrone, you, and I will live here."

Ray takes a deep breath and replies, "Everything is possible, honey. We both grew up in tin houses on the outskirts of town, and now we live in a story-building in the city center. Who says we won't be able to afford one of these mansions some day? We just need to keep on praying. Now, go in there, and do your job as well as you can. In the evening you can tell me everything about how those rich folks live."

Latoya starts work at the Millingtons' residence and is asked to prepare some tea and biscuits for Mrs. Millington and her lady friends. Latoya prepares everything meticulously to produce a good first impression and then discreetly walks into the living room to serve the guests. While she is serving the tea, Latoya overhears the conversation.

"Oh, dear," Mrs. Millington is telling her friends, "the economic slowdown in the United States is really having a toll on this island. My husband's hotel is now making losses, and he has had to fire so many employees because of that. What's even worse, my husband has had to take a large salary cut himself! As a result we can no longer afford to rent this house in Montego Bay. We will be moving to a cheaper place shortly. It is really unfortunate because I really enjoy living here, but things will remain tough in Jamaica until the US economy starts improving."

That evening Latoya returns home and tells Ray about the conversation she overheard at her employer's house. "Almighty Lord," Ray says, "so it turns out that rich folks are also struggling like we are. *That is no good*, honey. If the Millingtons can no longer afford to live in Montego Bay, then what chances do regular people like you and I have to make it there some day? We need to pray harder."

Key Concepts:

- Every economy goes through cycles. Periods of strong economic growth are generally associated with rising employment opportunities, rising wages and business profits, growing government revenues, and improvements in public services. In general, living standards for most people improve during periods of strong economic growth.

- On the other hand, when economic prospects are weak, unemployment tends to go up, and household incomes, business profits, and government revenues may come under pressure.

- Economic cycles are inevitable. However, government policies can help smooth the effects of cycles and create greater stability for households and businesses.

- We live in a globalized world where economies have become more interconnected. As a result, economic developments in one country can have knock-on effects on other nations.

3. PRODUCTIVITY: THE AFGHAN PISTACHIO FARMER

Ahmed Ahsan is a forty-five-year-old pistachio farmer from Samangan province in Afghanistan. He lives with his wife, Zaynab, his eighty-year-old father, and his nine children in a small clay house in the village of Aybak.

Aybak is a very small place, far away from everything, perched on the arid mountains of northern Afghanistan. It gets extremely hot in summer and very cold in winter. The main economic activities are pistachio farming, cattle herding, and mining from a nearby marble quarry.

Ahmed is the sole income earner in his family. He wakes up every day at six o'clock in the morning and starts working in the field. He grows pistachios, a delicious little nut that people use for making sweets. Growing pistachios is very hard work. It takes several weeks for the seeds to germinate and several years for the shrubs to turn into trees that produce nuts. Every day, Ahmed weeds out his orchard very carefully, shrub by shrub, making sure there are no insects near the roots or on the delicate leaves. He then goes back and forth to the nearby stream carrying heavy buckets full of water. He takes his time to irrigate the plants one by one and little by little. He does this twice a day, as the best way to water pistachio plants is to do it a drop at a time, to ensure the torrid sun does not damage them.

In the afternoons, Ahmed herds the family's sheep along the hills and valleys of Samangan. Because most of the land is arid, Ahmed needs to walk long distances to find patches of pasture that his sheep can graze on. He returns home exhausted at sunset and often asks himself as to what good is so much work for so little return, as he barely makes enough to feed everyone in his family. But what choice does he have? Who else can provide for his nine children? His elderly father with his limping leg? His wife Zaynab? No, these are thoughts he does not want to entertain.

Once a year, Ahmed harvests his pistachios, loads them into sacks, and places the sacks on the back of his donkey. He then walks several kilometers to the nearest town to sell his produce in the open market. On average, Ahmed sells one full sack of pistachios for 700 afghanis (the equivalent of 10 US dollars). Over the course of the year, his orchard yields about ten sacks. In total, Ahmed makes the equivalent of one hundred dollars a year from his pistachio orchard. He uses this money to buy winter clothes for his family, charcoal for his wife to prepare meals, and foodstuff, such as bread, tea, and sugar.

One day, Ahmed receives a parcel from his cousin Sherif, who lives in Kabul, the capital of Afghanistan. Sherif was born and raised in Aybak but moved to Kabul at the age of eighteen to pursue further education. He studied agricultural engineering at Kabul University and was now working for the Ministry of Agriculture. In the parcel, Sherif had included several batches of high-quality pistachio seeds from California. California, Sherif explained in his letter, was home to some of the world's largest commercial pistachio orchards. Over the years, they had invested a lot of resources in pistachio research and had developed a variety of seeds that were better suited to arid conditions. This new variety produced higher yields, was more resistant to plagues, and required less water. The new pistachio variety was now being promoted by the Ministry of Agriculture to increase farmers' productivity.

When he sees the pistachio seeds, Ahmed laughs with disbelief. He can't help but ask himself as to what good could anything American possibly be in the arid lands of Afghanistan. Things have always been the same in Samangan province since the beginnings of time and for as long as the village elders can remember. No, he does not believe in miracles happening on earth, or at least not in Samangan. So Ahmed decides against planting the new pistachio seeds.

When he returns home, Ahmed tells his wife about the Californian seeds he has received from his cousin Sherif and how he is planning to dispose of them. Zaynab bursts in anger and calls him a *donkey* for his resistance to new ideas. She insists that Ahmed plant the new pistachio seeds, arguing that it is worth a try. Ahmed reluctantly agrees and does as his wife suggests, as he does not like arguing.

A few years later, Ahmed wakes up to see a full field of pistachios as plump as he has ever seen in his lifetime! He harvests them and packs them into sacks. He can barely hold his breath in joy. He has managed to fill up twenty sacks—double his usual harvest! The pistachio plants have also grown faster than usual, and he has had to deal with fewer insect plagues and fewer trips to the stream.

So it turns out that his cousin Sherif was right: Californian seeds do miracles! Ahmed gives thanks to God and returns home from the market with 14,000 afghanis (the equivalent of 200 US dollars), twice the amount of money he usually makes. To celebrate this, he buys a silk scarf for his wife, a pair of new spectacles for his father, and a football for his children.

The people of Aybak soon realize that Ahmed's pistachio trees are growing much faster than theirs. So they approach him and ask him about his secret. Ahmed tells his fellow villagers everything about the Californian seeds and gives away a bunch of them so that everyone in the village can benefit from the new discovery.

The new seeds germinate rapidly, and the shrubs soon become luscious trees full of nuts. Over the following years, pistachio production in the village of Aybak increases significantly. And because the new plants are hardier and do not require as much watering and weeding, the villagers start having more time to engage in other productive activities.

Some villagers decide to plant potatoes and wheat in their spare time. Others plant grapes and pomegranates, and still some others decide to work at the nearby marble quarry to supplement their income. Overtime, the village of Aybak becomes one of the most prosperous villages in Samangan province, and it becomes well known all over the country for its pistachio orchards and its hospitable people.

Key Concepts:

- Productivity refers to how efficiently resources are employed in the production of goods and services.

- Productivity rises when a greater quantity of goods is produced in relation to the amount of resources employed. Productivity gains can be achieved through advances in technology and better management practices.

- Rising productivity leads to higher production and higher income levels, which in turn supports greater affordability and better living standards.

4. DEMAND AND SUPPLY: THE COLOMBIAN *HACIENDA* OWNER

Felipe Valencia is a thirty-five-year-old history professor at the Universidad de Los Andes in Bogota, the capital city of Colombia. Felipe spends most of his time writing research articles on Latin America's colonial history and its path to independence. In his free time, he enjoys reading the popular novels of Gabriel Garcia Marquez, one of his country's greatest writers.

Felipe was born and raised in his grandfather's *hacienda* (estate) in Valle del Cauca, a Colombian region close to the Pacific Ocean, where nature is abundant, land is fertile, and all men are romantic. That is the case, at least, of Don Alcides Caicedo, Felipe's maternal grandfather and the owner of the family's estate.

The two-hundred-hectare estate has been in the family for generations. Don Alcides inherited it from his father, Don Florentino, who in turn inherited it from his great-grandfather, Don Aureliano. Every stone in the *hacienda* tells a story, and it is in that very land that every descendant of the Caicedos was born and raised for the past four hundred years.

One day, Felipe arrives in his office and finds a letter on his desk. He instantly recognizes the elegant and slightly old-fashioned handwriting. As he tears the envelope open, the scent of the *hacienda* invades the room.

"My dear Grandson," Felipe reads, "I am no longer as young as I used to be. Yesterday morning, as I was sitting on the porch listening to the sounds of the early birds, a thought crossed my mind. It was as if the winds of the Pacific were whispering something to my ear—a sad and inevitable truth. I suddenly realized that it had been thirty years since I was last able to ride a horse! My knees hurt when the weather is damp and cold. My hands shake when they are not supposed to. As for my eyes, my dear Grandson, they cry when I least expect them to. You know the famous verse, *"Juventud, divino tesoro"* (youth is a divine treasure). Poets are always right. My youth has forever left me. At the ripe age of ninety-three, the time has come for me to pass onto you the keys of our estate. Leave everything behind: your research papers, your job, your girlfriends in Bogota! When I was your age, I too had all these and much more. But I left everything to devote my life to a greater calling: that of maintaining the legacy of our family's estate. Always yours, *Abuelito* (Grandpa)."

Felipe takes a deep breath. *Abuelito* is right. It is every respectable man's duty to honor his ancestors and engage in the noble quest of preserving the family's legacy. Yes, he is almost sure that Garcia Marquez would have written about it in one of his magical novels. Who is he, after all, to go against tradition? That same evening, Felipe writes his resignation letter. He leaves it in the dean's office, packs a few belongings, and takes a flight to Valle del Cauca.

When he reaches the *hacienda*, Don Alcides is waiting for him on the porch. He is wearing a large *sombrero* (straw hat) and a pair of pristine-white linen pants with a matching shirt. Don Alcides greets his grandson profusely, with tears in his eyes, thanking him for agreeing to take over the estate. "There is one more thing I need you to do, Felipe," he says. "You need to find yourself a wife, a good woman, like your grandmother was. Somebody who will iron your shirts, cook *empanadas* (traditional meat pies) for you, and assist you in the administration of the estate. You know the saying in our land: *behind every prosperous hacienda, there is a great woman*. You must get married. It is essential for the survival of our lineage and our estate. Since your grandmother died, may she rest in peace, things at the *hacienda* have gone from bad to worse. The workers steal the little I am able to produce, and our sugarcane and pineapple plantations have been disastrous. You must find a good woman, my grandson." Felipe takes another deep breath. *Abuelito* is right. It is time for him to get married.

The following Sunday, Felipe borrows Don Alcides' *sombrero*. He dresses in his white linen pants and matching shirt and walks to the Jesuit Mission of Santa Clara, which was established centuries ago by the Spaniards. Father Antonio receives him with a warm greeting. "What brings you to these lands, my son?" he asks.

"I am looking for a wife, Father," Felipe says timidly. "*Abuelito* suggested that the House of God may be the best place to find one."

"Come back tomorrow at this same time," Father Antonio says. "There is somebody I want you to meet."

The following day Felipe does as he was told. Father Antonio is waiting for him at the steps of the church, and with a gentle hand gesture, he makes the much-awaited introduction. "Meet Mercedes," he says.

The very moment he sees her, Felipe knows that he has found love. Mercedes has deep brown eyes and a mane of long black hair that falls beautifully on her waist. Her complexion is light brown, revealing that there is native blood in her veins. *Hermosa* (beautiful), Felipe thinks. He suddenly feels the urge to say something courteous, and he mutters the verses of some old poet. Mercedes smiles timidly, and for a second she covers her face graciously with her handkerchief. "She likes me," Felipe concludes.

After Mercedes has left, Felipe talks to Father Antonio in private. "She is one of the best women you could ever marry," Father Antonio assures him. "She is the only daughter in a family of twelve brothers. Chances are that she will give you plenty of boys to work on your land." Felipe seems content.

"And what about her cooking, Father?" he asks. "Do you think she can cook good *empanadas*?"

"Good?" Father replies. "The very best *empanadas* of the entire Valle del Cauca! I tasted them once when I was invited to her brother's engagement party."

"And what about ironing?" Felipe asks timidly. "Do you think she would be any good at it?"

"Don't be silly, my son!" Father exclaims. "Just look at her hands: they are those of a laborious woman."

Months later, Felipe marries Mercedes in a big celebration in the family's *hacienda*. They play *bambucos* (Colombian folk songs) and dance until the early hours of the morning. It does not take long for Felipe to realize that Father Antonio was right: Mercedes cooks the best *empanadas* of the entire Valle del Cauca. She is also good at ironing, but best of all, just like Don Alcides has hoped for, Mercedes is a great estate administrator. She keeps track of every expenditure, she ensures that workers do not steal, and she is able to explain why the price of such and such crop has changed from the previous year. Every so often, Mercedes would ask Felipe to sit next to her on the porch and go over the estate results. Mercedes would explain as follows:

Sugarcane: This year we made very little profits from our sugarcane plantation. Even though our harvest was as large as last year's, the price we achieved per ton was much lower. This is because Brazil, the world's largest producer of sugarcane, had a bumper harvest. As the world's supply of sugarcane increased, the global price of sugar declined, driving down prices for producers in Colombia and many other countries.

Pineapples: Our pineapple plantation is in losses this year. The market price of pineapples has declined so much that it is no longer sufficient to cover the cost of harvesting and transporting them to the market. Prices have collapsed as a result of a large increase in global supply coming from places such as the Philippines and Thailand. When there is a large increase in the supply of a product, prices fall.

Mangoes: The good news is that our mango plantation was very profitable this year. As you know, a juice factory recently opened in the region. The factory has started buying mangoes in large quantities from local suppliers. As the demand for mangoes has rapidly increased, the price of mangoes has gone up sharply. But mango prices may not remain this high forever. Farmers will react to high prices by increasing the size of their plantations. Overtime, as the supply of mangoes increases to meet demand, prices may fall back to more sustainable levels.

"It is all a matter of supply and demand, *cariño* (darling)," Mercedes concludes.

"*Abuelito* was right," Felipe says happily. "I am so glad I married you. Now let's go for a long horse ride along the mountains and valleys of our *hacienda*."

Key Concepts:

- The price of a product is determined by the interaction between buyers (demand) and sellers (supply). Demand is the amount of a particular good or service that consumers are willing and able to purchase at a given price. Supply refers to the quantity of goods or services that producers are willing to provide to the marketplace at a given price.

- Prices normally rise when there is a strong increase in demand for a product. Prices can also rise when there is a shortage (insufficient supply) of a good.

- Prices tend to fall when demand for a product declines or when there is excess supply of a good.

- Prices change overtime to bring demand and supply into balance. For example, when there is a large increase in demand, prices rise to encourage suppliers to produce more in order to meet the higher level of consumer appetite.

- On the other hand, when there is excess supply of a good, prices tend to fall. The lower price puts pressure on suppliers to cut back on production and also encourages consumers to buy more.

5. Price-Setting Mechanism: The Pakistani Businessman

Suleiman Habib, aged forty-eight, is one of the most prominent businessmen in Pakistan. Suleiman is the chairman and chief executive officer of Habib Holdings, one of the country's largest group of companies. Over generations of family ownership, Habib Holdings has amassed vast amounts of wealth and obtained control of some of the country's most reputable businesses. In fact, Habib Holdings owns the well-known Pakistani Sandal Company, the fast-food chain Indus Kebab Express, the cloth manufacturer Textile Assembly Co., in addition to one of the country's largest commercial banks and newspaper printing presses.

Suleiman lives in Karachi, the country's largest city, in a twelve-bedroom residence that he shares with his parents, his wife, Amina, and their vast array of domestic helpers, gardeners, and security guards. Suleiman considers himself a lucky man. He has what most wealthy men in his social circle dream of: a brand-new Porsche Cayenne, a private jet that he uses to fly to Dubai on shopping holidays, and, best of all, a beautiful, young wife.

In his free time, Suleiman enjoys playing polo with his friends. But for several weeks now, a problem—a business problem—has been keeping him from indulging in this hobby. Indeed, nothing upsets Suleiman more than business issues. He is good at dealing with domestic emergencies, such as getting the water tank refilled when it runs out of water, resolving petty disputes between his gardeners, and calming Amina down when she is upset at him for coming home late. But when it comes to business issues, it is different. They cling onto Suleiman's mind and do not let him rest until he has managed to resolve them.

Suleiman's problem has to do with Pakistan's electricity supply, or, more appropriately, the lack of it. Indeed, just like in many other developing nations, electricity supply in Pakistan is highly unreliable, and blackouts are a common feature of daily life. For the past months, blackouts have been more frequent and prolonged than usual, and this is having a negative impact on the financial performance of Habib Holdings.

Most of Suleiman's businesses rely on electricity to operate. Suleiman needs electricity to operate the large industrial machinery that manufactures sandals and assembles clothes. He also needs electricity to run the refrigerators and air conditioners of his fast-food outlets and to run the newspaper printing press.

Because electricity shortages are frequent in the country, Suleiman has already invested in a diesel-fueled generator to back up his operations. Diesel generators are good at generating power, but they are very expensive to run. They keep on sucking diesel oil, and before you realize, your costs would have gone out of control. This is exactly what is happening now to Habib Holdings. When Suleiman receives the company's last set of financial results, its profits have halved because of escalating power costs!

One morning, Suleiman receives a wedding invite from his childhood friend, Daud Omrani. Daud and Suleiman studied together at the reputable Karachi Grammar School, but since their graduation, their lives have taken very different routes. While Suleiman took over his family's business, Daud followed his uncle's footsteps into politics and was now serving as the country's energy minister.

"Wear your best *saree* (traditional Pakistani cloth), Amina," Suleiman suggests. "We are going to Daud's wedding. Everyone you can think of will be there!" As they reach the wedding venue, Suleiman feels a tinge of jealously: this is probably the most lavish and luxurious wedding party he has ever attended! There are colorful flowers and lanterns everywhere; golden, silver, and red cushions beautifully arranged; and the most delicious sweets and mango *lassis* (yogurt-based drink) being served.

Suleiman goes up to his friend Daud and greets him fondly. "Long time, my friend!" Daud exclaims. "I have not seen you playing polo in a while. What has been keeping you so busy?" Suleiman explains to his friend the most recent business problems he is having and how the energy crisis in the country is having a negative impact on his companies.

It is perhaps not appropriate, Suleiman thinks, to talk business on such a special occasion, but since Daud is the country's energy minister, he might be able to provide some explanation on what is going on.

"My friend," Daud says. "As the energy minister, I am facing a big dilemma. As you know, Pakistan is a big country with a population of over 180 million people. Of all these people, not everyone is as wealthy as we are, and not everyone can pay market prices for electricity. One of our government's policies is to put a ceiling on the price that our main electricity provider can charge. That way, the majority of people, including the poorest, can afford to run a refrigerator, charge their mobile phones, or simply turn on their lights. But the big dilemma is the following: as you know we suffer major blackouts because not enough electricity is being produced. Our government often meets with the state's electricity producer and pleads for an increase in production in order to address this shortage. But the electricity company always refuses and provides the same excuse: the regulated price of electricity is capped at such a low level that they do not generate sufficient profits to be able to fund new electricity-production facilities. That is why electricity shortages persist!"

"I see," Suleiman says. "And why can't our government just remove the price cap and let electricity prices shoot up? This will incentivize producers to build new power plants, and it will also help businesses like my own. You see, my friend, I would really like to expand my sandal factory, but given the current power situation, I cannot afford to do so," Suleiman explains.

"You have not changed a bit since our school days, Suleiman," Daud laughs. "If we do what you say, millions of people won't be able to afford electricity at all. There is a trade-off to consider. Politics is not a game for the fainthearted. But please, my friend, come and taste some of these sweets. Just take a seat somewhere, and enjoy the wedding. The dancing is about to start."

Key Concepts:

- In a market where buyers and sellers are allowed to interact freely, the price of a product adjusts to bring demand and supply into balance.

- Market distortions, such as oversupplies or product shortages, can occur when prices are not allowed to adjust freely.

- For example, when a government intervenes in a market to set the price of a good below its normal level, this can create a product shortage. At lower-than-normal prices, suppliers are discouraged from producing more. At the same time, the lower-than-normal price encourages greater consumer demand, creating an even larger shortage.

- There are certain situations when price interventions can lead to more optimal results. For instance, when there is not enough competition in a market, a few powerful suppliers can set prices at higher-than-normal levels. In such cases, government regulation can be beneficial in bringing prices down to normal levels and ensuring adequate supply.

6. Response to Price Changes: The Japanese Retired Accountant

Mizue Kasuga is a sixty-five-year-old retired accountant from Tokyo, the capital city of Japan. She lives in a small apartment located on the twentieth floor of a skyscraper in the city's commercial district. Mizue has a grandson, Akihiro, who often spends the weekends with her.

This weekend is Akihiro's tenth birthday, and Mizue has baked him a chocolate-and-strawberry cake. As Akihiro is about to blow the candles, Mizue interrupts him, "Akihiro, my grandson, on your birthday I wish you a prosperous and long life. I hope that you grow up to become a great cook and a great accountant just like your grandmother!"

Akihiro laughs and replies, "Grandma, cooking and accounting are not subjects that are taught at school. So I can only make your wish come true if you teach me!"

"I certainly will," Grandma Mizue replies.

The following day Grandma wakes Akihiro up early in the morning. "Wash your face, and get dressed, Akihiro, we are going to the market," she says. "Today, I will teach you how to roll sushi and in the process, you will also learn the basic principles of financial planning."

"But it is too early, Grandma," Akihiro complains.

"Do as I say, Grandson," Grandma replies.

As they walk to the market, Grandma starts telling Akihiro, "To become a good accountant, you need to start by applying certain basic principles to your daily life. It is essential that you learn how to plan ahead and pay attention to detail—no cheating, no cutting corners. Great accountants have to be balanced people—trustworthy and meticulous."

"Every week," Grandma continues, "you need to prepare a budget of your spending. Then you must stick to it religiously, keeping track of every item you buy and ensuring you never spend more than you planned to. On the first day of every month, when I receive my pension, I plan how I am going to spend that money in advance. I allocate some money to pay my rent, my groceries, and my utility bills. And I always set some money aside in case any unforeseen emergency arises. It is good to be prudent and save for the rainy days. Shame on me if I ever have to borrow money! Learning how to live within one's means is essential!"

"Exercising self-control is the hardest part," Grandma continues as she notices Akihiro is staring at a juice stand. "If you suddenly feel thirsty, you may have to forgo buying that juice if it had not been planned for in your budget. At the end of the day, you want your accounts to balance. You don't want to have expenses that are larger than your income just because of some silly aloe-vera juice, right?" she asks. "Accountants need to be reliable, predictable, and exact."

Akihiro listens carefully and nods. Grandma's words make a lot of sense to him, but he does not like the part about forgoing aloe-vera juice. Does a child really need to make that sacrifice in order to become a great accountant in the future? Would he be cutting corners if he skipped that one little rule? And would Grandma ever find out, in the first place?

When they reach the market, Grandma approaches a fish stand and asks the fishmonger what the price of salmon is. "1,200 yen (equivalent of 10 US dollars)!" Grandma exclaims. "That is too expensive! Please serve me some tuna instead. It is cheaper than salmon, and the sushi will taste just as good," she says.

Grandma explains to Akihiro that the price of fish varies from day to day according to how abundant the catch has been. On good days when fishermen manage to catch a lot of salmon, the price of salmon is cheap. However, on days when the catch is scarce, prices become more expensive. When that happens, Grandma buys cheaper alternatives, such as tuna. "Consumers are sensitive to price changes," she says. "Price information helps us make choices and budget our spending," she concludes.

After shopping, Akihiro and Grandma return home and start preparing sushi rolls. Grandma takes her time to teach Akihiro how to slice the fish, chop the avocado, prepare the sticky rice, and put everything together carefully into sturdy rolls. Once the meal is ready, Akihiro and Grandma sit down to savor the food and sip a cup of green tea.

After the meal, Akihiro turns on the television to watch some cartoons, while Grandma sits down next to him to do some knitting. Grandma is using five different wool yarns and is mixing and matching them diligently at a very fast pace. "You are so talented Grandma," Akihiro says. "I am amazed at how fast you can knit. But what are you knitting?"

Grandma explains to Akihiro that old people sometimes get bored or stressed and when that happens they take up hobbies, such as knitting, that help them relax and pass their time. She then adds that she is knitting baby suits. "Baby suits?" Akihiro repeats very surprised. "But there are no babies in our family," he says. "So who will wear those baby suits? They will be too small for me."

Grandma explains that she supplies the hand-knit baby suits to a nearby shop, which then retails them to customers. "How much money do you get for every suit, Grandma?" Akihiro asks. "And how many do you produce every week?"

"Well, it is a funny story," Grandma says. "Initially, when I entered into an agreement with the shop, they agreed to pay me 600 yen (equivalent of 5 US dollars) for every baby suit I knitted. I was producing about ten a week. Then one day I was walking by the shop and realized that the owner was Mr. Kaga, one of my childhood friends from Kyoto. He invited me over for tea, and we spent hours reminiscing about our school days. Before leaving, he told me that my baby suits were of very fine quality and that, as a result, he would increase the price he paid me to 1,000 yen per unit (equivalent of 8 US dollars). He had always been such a kind man, Mr. Kaga!" Grandma sighs. "The higher price as well as my loyalty to him motivated me to spend more time knitting every week. And so, at the moment, I produce about twenty baby suits a week," she concludes.

Akihiro laughs. "That is another example of how prices help us make choices, Grandma," he says. "You reacted to a change in price just like you did earlier this morning with the price of salmon and tuna."

"Indeed," Grandma says. "I am very pleased to know that you are learning so fast, Akihiro. In only one day, you have learned about financial planning and sushi. Tomorrow, I shall get you started on knitting."

Key Concepts:

- Consumers react to price changes by adapting their levels of demand. In general, when the price of a good falls, people want to buy more of it (demand increases). On the other hand, when the price of a good rises, consumers tend to buy less of it.

- Producers also react to price changes by adapting their levels of supply. When the price of a good increases, producers are encouraged to supply more goods to the marketplace.

- Price information helps consumers make choices based on their needs and their affordability. It also helps suppliers make decisions regarding which goods to produce and in which quantity.

7. Purchasing Power: The Ghanaian Cocoa Farmer

Kwesi Appiah is a forty-two-year-old farmer from Berekuso, a small village in the eastern region of Ghana. Kwesi lives in a spacious compound house on Berekuso's main road, along with his wife, Ama, his three children, and his brother-in-law. Kwesi's family has lived in Berekuso for as long as anyone can remember. They live comfortably there, surrounded by their relatives, and in harmony with nature.

Berekuso is located in the lush Akwapim Hills. It enjoys tropical weather all year long and is blessed with abundant rainfall that provides water for farming and basic household needs. The village lies in a tranquil valley overlooking a magnificent green scenery.

"Our land is our greatest treasure," Kwesi's grandfather taught him when he was a child. "Mother Nature carries in her womb the seeds to the most delicious fruits that men can eat. Everything grows here: plantains, mangoes, papayas, pineapples, cocoa, and eggplants. *Man* carries the key to nature's treasure. If *man* is hungry, he just needs to stretch his arm and pull out of the earth a succulent yam. If *man* is thirsty, he can pluck a ripe coconut, crack it open, and drink its delicious water. As for food," Grandpa had concluded, "it is abundant in our land. We shall never go hungry."

Kwesi thinks that Grandpa was one of the wisest men he has ever met. He was a village elder, after all, and age had to count for something. Over the years, Grandpa's words have proven to be right: Kwesi and his family have never lacked food.

Kwesi owns a small cocoa plantation that he shares with his brother-in-law. Twice a year, the two men harvest the cocoa pods, sell them in the market, and divide the proceeds. On the side, Kwesi also farms plantains, corn, cassava, tomatoes, and spinach. "Farming many different crops will ensure you always have something to eat or sell," Grandpa had taught Kwesi.

Kwesi's wife, Ama, runs a small shop on the main Berekuso road. She sells foodstuff, such as canned sardines, corned beef, Lipton tea, and Maggie cubes, and also toiletries, such as toothpaste, shea butter, and deodorant spray. Together, Kwesi and Ama make about 400 cedis a month (the equivalent of 100 US dollars). This is more than enough to pay for their children's school fees and uniforms, buy new clothes for special occasions, and send some money every month to Ama's father, who lives far away and is too old to farm.

One day, Kwesi receives a visitor, Francis Mensah, his long-estranged cousin who migrated to the United Kingdom several years back. Francis arrives unexpectedly and gets off the noisy *trotro* (minibus) on the main Berekuso road. He is carrying a large suitcase.

"*Akwaaba* (welcome)!" Kwesi shouts when he sees his relative from afar. "Welcome home." Kwesi inspects his cousin carefully. He looks him up and down several times, and then proceeds to say, "Francis, my brother, you are looking more and more like a *white man*, wearing those short trousers that make you look like a school boy!"

"Ah, brother," Francis explains, "ever since I moved to London, my body has gotten so used to the cold weather that I can no longer withstand the heat of Africa." Kwesi laughs frantically. He holds his cousin's luggage, and walks him to his compound house, where he assumes Francis is coming to stay.

The two cousins sit down in the garden, under the shade of a mango tree. After a short conversation, Kwesi points at Francis' luggage. "What presents have you brought us from the United Kingdom, my brother? Any cooking pots or pans? Sport shoes for my sons? Some nice fluffy towels for our bath? Please open your luggage so that we may see what is in there."

As Kwesi is speaking, his wife Ama overhears the conversation and feels the need to intervene. "Oh, Kwesi," she adds, "it is not good manners to urge a visitor like that. He must be tired from the trip. Let him do it at his own time."

"Why not?" Kwesi asks, "He is rich, and we are poor. And besides, we are relatives, so he should share with us some of his wealth. *Sharing is caring*, as we were taught in Berekuso Primary School. Have you forgotten?"

Francis reluctantly opens his luggage and takes out a small box of toffee that he hands to Kwesi. "Toffee?", Kwesi says slightly disappointed. "After all these years abroad, all you bring is a box of toffee?"

When he hears this, Francis becomes furious. His eyes turn red, and the veins on his forehead swell as if they are about to burst with anger. He has changed a lot, Francis, since he moved to the United Kingdom. He is no longer the laid-back fellow he once was—carefree and joyful.

"I have not brought anything else for you or your family, Kwesi," Francis retorts. "Nothing else," he insists. "All I have is a story. I want to tell you about my life in London," he continues. "But first, call your children so that they may also hear this. Actually, please summon everyone in the village of Berekuso, the neighbors, the Chief, and even the Queen Mother! Everybody should sit under this mango tree and listen to my story—the story of Francis Mensah who traveled abroad."

"I left Berekuso twelve years ago. It was one of those cool mornings in the rainy season. The entire village came out to see me off. As I was waiting for the *trotro* that would take me to the airport, everybody came forward to wish me well and give me a last piece of advice. 'You will sweat in hell but chill in heaven,' my mate Kojo had warned me, referring to the well-known fact that as a migrant in the United Kingdom, I would have to work very hard in exchange for the right to retire a rich man in Berekuso and build a mansion for my family. 'As soon as you reach London,' my sweetheart had pleaded, 'send me some British pounds so that I can set up the very first forex bureau in the village.' 'Go out there, and take care of me,' Mama had requested, 'the same way I took care of you when you were growing up.'"

"I boarded the dusty *trotro* and caught a glimpse of my relatives and friends one last time. I could see excitement and hope in people's faces, even jealousy. I then looked at Mama one last time, and that popular song came to my mind. I stuck my head out of the *trotro*'s window and sang loudly: '*Sweet mother, I no go forget you, for dey suffer way you suffer for me* (Sweet Mother, I will not forget you for the way you suffered for me).' Everybody laughed, and I sailed off. When I looked back, Berekuso was just a small dot in the horizon."

"I arrived in the United Kingdom full of youthful dreams and expectations. 'Life is good in Europe,' my older brother had assured me. 'You will make *plenty money*,' my mother had hoped. 'You will become a big man,' my sister had anticipated."

"I soon found a job as a taxi driver. Before I traveled, my mate Kojo had told me that a taxi driver in the United Kingdom could make as much money in one day as a farmer in Berekuso makes in a full month! That thought alone kept me going through those foggy days abroad. My mate was right. On a good day, I can make as much as 200 pounds driving my taxi around London. On average, I make about 1,500 pounds a month."

"That is a fortune!" Ama exclaims clapping her hands energetically. "If I had that money in Berekuso, I would send my children to private school, open a bigger shop, set up a fish farm, and sew a new dress every week!"

"That is the whole point," Francis interrupts. "The story does not take place in Berekuso but in London, and 1,500 pounds there do not take you as far as they do in this village! Listen carefully, everyone. Children, take note: there will be a math question at the end. I make 1,500 pounds a month, but I need to pay a monthly rent of 800 pounds. This is the cheapest rent I can afford for a small *chamber and hall* (one bedroom apartment) in a deprived area on the outskirts of London. Then there is the cost of transport for my children to take the bus to school every morning: it comes up to about 150 pounds a month. I also have to pay for heating, gas, and electricity. You cannot just use charcoal to cook in the United Kingdom. This costs another 200 pounds a month. I spend another 300 pounds to buy groceries at the supermarket and pay for my mobile phone and council tax bills. What do the numbers add up to? Anyone?"

"One thousand four hundred fifty pounds!" a school boy shouts diligently.

"That's right," Francis says. "I earn 1,500 pounds a month as a taxi driver in London, working over fourteen hours a day! That is longer than any farmer works in Berekuso! I then have to spend about 1,450 pounds on basic living expenses. This means that I am left with only fifty pounds at the end of every month! I barely make any savings, and I often need to borrow money to pay my bills."

When he hears these words, Kwesi feels a sudden rush of shame. He feels the urge to stand up in the middle of the crowd that has gathered under the mango tree and apologize publicly to his cousin Francis. This will be a good way, he thinks, to highlight the morale of the story and make sure that the children will take away a lesson. That was exactly the way that elders liked to teach children in Africa: by telling them stories that they could relate to.

"My brother," Kwesi says, "I am sorry I was so rude to you when I asked for presents. I wrongly assumed that you were rich and I was poor. I did not know about your living conditions in London. It is only now, after I hear your story, that I realize that I am the rich man and you are the poor one. My grandfather was right: our land, Berekuso, is our treasure."

Key Concepts:

- Purchasing power, or affordability, refers to the quantity of goods and services that a given amount of income can buy. People are most concerned with the affordability that their income provides (relative purchasing power) than with the actual amount of money they earn (absolute level of income).

- The purchasing power of one dollar of income varies across different countries (or within regions in a country) because the price of many goods is influenced by local cost considerations.

- Comparing wage levels across countries or regions can be misleading because wages on their own do not fully reflect affordability levels in a given location. While one dollar of income can afford many goods in a Ghanaian village, it can barely afford a bottle of water in London.

- In order to appropriately assess affordability levels across regions, it is important to compare income levels to the cost of an average consumption basket locally (including items such as housing, food, education, and transportation).

8. COMPETITION AND LIVING STANDARDS: THE MOROCCAN SOFTWARE ENGINEER

Rachid Benchekroun is a software engineer from Casablanca, Morocco's largest city. Rachid works for a technology company developing computer games and lives in an elegant villa around the *corniche* (waterfront promenade), one of Casablanca's fanciest neighborhoods. But life has not always been easy for Rachid, and at the age of twenty-five, he feels that he has come a long way in life.

Rachid grew up in Casablanca's suburbs, in a small one-bedroom apartment that he shared with his parents, his three siblings, and two of his cousins from the village. Abdel Karim, Rachid's father, was a mechanic, while his mother, Fatima, was a homemaker. From an early age, Rachid learned the value of hard work. He attended school in the mornings and helped his father in the garage in the afternoons, oiling engines and pumping tires. At night, Rachid did his school homework diligently under a kerosene lamp. "Study hard, young boy," his father often reminded him, "for it is the only way that the son of a mechanic from Chefchaouen can become someone in life."

"*Inshallah* (God willing), someday you will become an engineer," his mother Fatima hoped. "You will make your uncles proud."

Rachid did as he was told. He studied diligently and soon became the best student in his class. He earned a scholarship to study at the Lycée Lyautée, a prestigious French school in town, and upon completing his baccalaureate, he got accepted into an engineering program at the Sorbonne University in Paris. "*Mashallah* (praise the Lord)," his mother exclaimed when she heard the news. "Go to France, and make us proud *habibi* (my dear)!" And once again, Rachid did as he was told.

But living and studying in Paris was never meant to be easy for the fourth child of Fatima and Abdel Karim Benchekroun. Paris was, Rachid thought, colder and damper than the refrigerator of a butcher's shop. People ran everywhere all the time. They never stopped to greet one another or ask about their relatives, and there was little time to enjoy the small pleasures of life. Rachid missed his hometown, Casablanca, the tranquil evening walks by the ocean, and the regular calls to prayer that paced every day's life. He also missed wandering around the narrow streets of the *medina* (old town), the scent of mint tea, the soothing sea breeze, and the brightness of the Mediterranean sun. But above all, Rachid missed his mother's *harira* soup (lentil soup) and the sound of his father's voice while he used to oil engines.

"I shall return to my homeland when I complete my studies," Rachid promised himself shortly after arriving in France. But his mother, Fatima, was not happy to hear about this decision. "*Habibi*," she said over the phone, "your father and I have thought about it, and Paris is good for you. You should remain there." Rachid felt heartbroken after hearing these words. On what basis could his mother give such a piece of advice when she had never traveled outside of her hometown? Did she know anything about Paris? Did she know how heavy his heart was feeling and how much he was craving for her *harira* soup?

Graduation day arrived, and Rachid finally got his engineering degree from the Sorbonne University. Shortly afterward, he did as he vowed he would. He returned to Casablanca despite his mother's wishes. He knew it would not be easy finding a suitable job in his hometown, but he would try his best. "*Maktoub* (it is written)," Rachid told himself, "there is no point being anxious about the future, for only God knows what is written in every man's destiny." Several months later, Rachid got a job at a software company developing computer games. He soon settled into his new life and rented an elegant villa around the *corniche*. Paris was now a distant memory, but a part of him was still there.

"Michelle *hayati* (my life)," Rachid mumbles on his evening walks around the sea. He is referring to a beautiful French girl that he fell in love with while he was studying in Paris. They took several courses together, and at times they shared an afternoon tea and a stroll around the city. But Rachid never mustered the courage to reveal his feelings to her. He was not good at these sorts of things, and he was not sure it was the right thing to do. "She will take you for granted," his cousin Faouzi warned him, "and then she will go away with another man who plays harder to get."

Perhaps Faouzi was right. And then there was the question of whether Michelle would ever want to move to Casablanca to be with him. "She will not last long here," Faouzi anticipated. But Rachid's feelings did not change because of his cousin's premonitions. "*Maktoub*," Rachid told himself, "only God knows what is meant to happen in every man's life."

One evening, Rachid reads the popular story of Leila and Majnoun, an ancient tale similar to that of Romeo and Juliet. "I shall be Majnoun," he tells himself after reading the book, "and Michelle shall be Leila." And because Rachid is a man of his word, he promises himself that he will not rest until he wins over Michelle's heart. He has made up his mind: he will travel to Paris several times a month to visit his beloved, and overtime he will reveal his feelings to her. It does not matter what cousin Faouzi thinks of the matter.

That same evening, Rachid goes online to buy a plane ticket to Paris. After doing some research, he realizes that in order to fly directly from Morocco to France, he only has one choice: flying Sahara Air, the country's only air carrier that is allowed to operate on that route. The average price of a round-trip ticket is 6,000 Moroccan dirhams (the equivalent of 600 US dollars). "That is almost half of my monthly income," Rachid thinks. "The cost of flying is so high that I won't be able to travel as often as I would like to," he ponders. But could something as beautiful as the love of Leila and Majnoun be jeopardized because of the cost of air travel?

Over the following months, the government of Morocco decides to lift the regulatory restrictions that were preventing other carriers from flying on the Casablanca–Paris route. This dismantles Sahara Air's monopoly and opens the door for competition. All of a sudden, a large number of new airlines start offering cheap flights to France. One of such airlines is Desert Fly, a low-cost company offering round-trip tickets for as little as 500 dirhams (50 US dollars), a fraction of the price that Sahara Air was charging. "*Mashallah*," Rachid tells himself. "Now I can afford to see Michelle every weekend if I wish to."

Rachid meets his cousin Faouzi for tea and tells him about the cheap deals that Desert Fly is offering to fly to France. "Your joy is somebody else's unhappiness," Faouzi retorts. "My friend Mounira is a flight attendant with Sahara Air, the former monopoly and she is very upset about the arrival of new competition. Her salary has just been halved, and she has been asked to work twice the amount of hours per week! Her boss explained to her that the only way the company can survive is by lowering their fares. But in order to do this, the company needs to lower its cost base. This means they have to lay off some employees and cut salaries across the company."

"Those are terrible news," Rachid says, while he pauses to sip on his mint tea.

"On the other hand," Faouzi continues, "I read in the newspaper that the low-cost airline Desert Fly has just opened its headquarters here in Casablanca. This has created over one thousand new jobs in the city. In fact, my friend Khaled, who had been unemployed for several years, has just been hired to work for them. He is really grateful to have found a job!"

"*Mashallah*," Rachid adds.

That evening, on his way back home, Rachid walks around the *corniche* enjoying the fresh ocean breeze. Suddenly, an idea crosses his mind, "I shall fly to Paris this weekend and propose to Michelle." Then he hesitates and starts considering the different scenarios that could result from such a bold move. "Will she accept and throw herself into my arms?" he wonders, "or, will she refuse and slap my face?" All of a sudden, the Atlantic winds blow strongly, and Rachid feels as if someone is whispering something in his ear. "*Maktoub*," he hears, "only God knows what is written in every man's destiny."

Key Concepts:

- Businesses are set up to make profits. When there is little or no competition (few suppliers), businesses can raise prices substantially and earn large profits at the expense of customers.

- Competition provides consumers with choice and puts pressure on companies to deliver better products at more attractive prices. Competition is essential in order to align the profit-seeking goal of businesses to the welfare of consumers.

- In a market where there are many suppliers (a competitive market), the companies that earn the largest profits are usually the ones that deliver the best value to customers. Competition creates incentives for businesses to become more efficient, improve their product offerings, and lower prices.

9. INTERNATIONAL TRADE: THE SPANISH CARPENTER

Enrique Silva is a fifty-two-year-old carpenter and businessman from Olula del Rio, a small village in the south of Spain. His company employs over fifty people and sells furniture all over the country. Because Enrique's business is one of the most prominent in the region, many people consider him a wealthy man. That makes Enrique proud, but deep inside of him, he knows the truth. "I am not rich," Enrique often reminds himself. "I am just a poor man with money."

Enrique will never forget his childhood and its hardships. He grew up in a *cortijo* (an isolated farm) on the outskirts of Olula. Being the eleventh son of a farming family, he remembers going to bed with an empty stomach and dreaming that he was feasting over a large platter of succulent cured meat and delicious bread loaves. Back then, his family's main diet consisted of boiled potatoes and onions, and they often snacked on dried fruits and nuts to keep hunger away.

"Olives and almonds! That is all that can grow on this barren land!" Mama Anica, Enrique's grandmother, often complained. "Any time I am lucky enough to grow cauliflowers or artichokes," she continued, "torrential rains flood my land and ruin my harvest! Last time when this happened, I was woken up in the early hours by my neighbor. 'Wake up, Mama Anica,' the neighbor had said, 'for you went to bed rich and you have woken up poor!' The neighbor was right about something—we are condemned to wake up poor," Mama Anica used to tell Enrique.

"You should do like your cousins," Mama Anica told Enrique when he turned sixteen. "Emigrate to Germany or Switzerland. Over there," she continued, "you will be able to make a living and lift us out of poverty."

But Enrique strongly rejected his grandmother's suggestions. "We may be poor, Mama Anica, but I will never leave this land," he replied firmly. "I have made a pledge to San Sebastian, the patron saint of Olula, that I will never leave this village."

"Amen," Mama Anica said when she heard this, which is what she usually said when she did not want to enter into an argument. However, inside of her, she lamented that her grandson was stubborn like a mule.

Since the day that Enrique rejected his grandmother's suggestion of going abroad, he decided to devote his life to carpentry, working humbly and diligently. Over the years, life in Olula got better for everyone, but one thing remained of the old times: those centenary olive trees with their twisted trunks, reminding people of the past.

As the village got wealthier, people started building new houses, and Enrique's furniture business prospered. He was able to hire more people to work for him, build a new manufacturing plant, and buy several trucks to deliver furniture across the country. Business was thriving, until one day, things changed for the worse.

"What is going on, Brother Enrique?" his sister Ana asks him one Sunday in church. "I know you are a pious man, but over the past days, you have spent longer than usual in church, and your face seems to be concealing some problem."

"You are right, Sister," Enrique confesses. "There is something worrying me. It has to do with my furniture business. Over the past months, my sales have declined, and I am struggling to pay my employees' wages. I need a miracle to avoid having to fire some of my workers!"

"It is all because of globalization and greater competition," Enrique continues. "I have noticed that a lot of shops are now selling easy-to-assemble furniture imported from China. It is not as beautiful and durable as the one I produce, but it costs a fraction of the price, and consumers like cheap things!" he laments.

"It is hard for me to match those prices," Enrique says. "The cost of labor and materials in China is much cheaper than it is here in Spain," he continues. As he is saying this, Enrique looks up and sees the image of San Sebastian, the patron saint of Olula. Suddenly, an idea crosses his mind. He would find ways to reduce his cost base—by importing cheaper materials from abroad and producing a new line of affordable furniture that could compete with the self-assembly sets that consumers are buying.

Later that day, on his way back home, Enrique meets his cousin Candida who has recently recovered from a rare illness. "Thank God for your recovery, Cousin," Enrique tells her. "I prayed so much for you, and San Sebastian finally listened to my prayers."

"You are right," Candida says. "While your prayers must have helped, we also need to give thanks to international trade! The doctor told me that I owe my recovery to a drug that was discovered last year by a Canadian pharmaceutical company. He explained that it costs a huge amount of money to research the cure for a rare disease like the one I had and that companies are only incentivized to fund the research because they can amortize their investment by selling the drug to a larger global market. If there was no trade between nations and companies were restricted to selling products within their nation's borders, such investments would not take place. And I may not be alive right now," she concludes.

"You are right, Cousin," Enrique says. "It is also thanks to international trade that nowadays we have access to so many things that were once a luxury. See those cars, for instance, or those tractors, or those mobile phones. Just a few decades ago, these goods were so expensive that they were only within the reach of a few. But overtime, as the world's economy has become more integrated, greater competition has led to productivity gains in many industries. As a result, consumer goods have become cheaper and more accessible. Producers have to work harder to compete in a global market, but in return, they have the opportunity to sell their products around the world," he concludes.

That same evening, Enrique starts devising strategies to turn his business around. He goes online and contacts a list of international suppliers that can provide him with the materials and tools he needs to deliver self-assembly furniture sets like the ones that consumers are buying.

Months later, Enrique starts seeing the benefits of his new strategy. His company's sales recover and his new range of furniture is so well received that he even gets new orders from as far as Argentina and Chile. This is the first time that Enrique sells his products abroad, and he starts considering the possibility of opening a new sales office in Latin America.

Enrique feels that somewhere up there, in the deep blue sky of Olula, above the centenary olive trees, San Sebastian, the patron saint, is smiling at him.

"Thank you, Lord," he says humbly.

Key Concepts:

- Greater economic interaction among nations (international trade) contributes to higher levels of innovation and productivity in many industries.

- International trade increases sales opportunities for companies and creates stronger incentives for firms to invest in product innovation.

- International trade intensifies competition among firms. In this larger market, companies that are able to deliver the most attractive products at compelling prices have the opportunity to earn substantial profits. On the other hand, firms that are less innovative and less efficient may struggle to remain in business.

- Consumers around the world stand to benefit from international trade as it enhances consumer choice and promotes better value for money.

10. INFLATION: THE ARGENTINIAN STUDENT

Josefina Bustamante is a twenty-one-year-old art student from Buenos Aires, the capital city of Argentina. Josefina lives with her father and her seven siblings in Recoleta, an upscale neighborhood where many fashionable shops and trendy restaurants are located. Josefina's father, Don Amancio, works for AgricGlobal, a large agricultural company that exports Argentinian soybean and beef to many countries around the world.

As a student, Josefina receives from her father a monthly stipend of 2,000 pesos (the equivalent of 150 US dollars). Josefina uses this stipend to pay for her metro pass, buy books for university, go out for coffees with her friends, and occasionally treat herself to little luxuries. Once a month, she likes going to movies with her boyfriend, Andres.

Josefina's stipend is more than enough for her to do everything she wants and even make some savings. At the end of every month, Josefina always sets some money aside in a white envelope that she stores safely in her room. Once a year, during summer break, she uses these savings to go on a motorbike trip with Andres. Last year, the couple visited the Patagonia region, in what they remember to be the most beautiful trip of their lives. Next year, they are planning to visit the famous Iguazu Falls, but in order to afford that, they need to save a bit more.

The end of the month approaches, and Josefina realizes that she has been unable to make any savings toward her upcoming trip. She wonders why that is. She has not done anything special this month, and her spending habits have not changed. She ponders over it but is unable to find an answer. "Money flies," she tells herself and moves on with her day.

Weeks later, Josefina runs out of money once again. But this time, it happens midway through the month. When Andres phones her to invite her to the cinema, she excuses herself saying that she will not be able to pay for it. "*Che* (Argentinian slang for 'hey') Josefina," Andres says, "what are boyfriends for? Come along, I will treat you." But Josefina kindly refuses as she has been taught by her father that she should never accept gifts that she cannot return.

A few weeks later, Josefina runs out of money once again. This time it happens just ten days after she receives her monthly stipend. Josefina no longer has enough money to buy coffee after class, and it has been several months that she has not been able to go to the cinema with Andres. "There is something fishy going on here," she tells herself. "Everybody knows that money flies, but these pesos of mine are flying away too quickly! What on earth is going on? I need to find out," she concludes. So she decides to take a little notebook and keep a detailed diary of her expenditure over the following weeks.

Months later, Josefina sits down in the living room with her little notebook and a calculator. She starts punching numbers frantically, scribbling on the side of her notebook. She scratches her head several times and uses her hands to twist her long hair repeatedly. Then she realizes that the price of items she has been buying has gone up by about 30 percent since she started keeping track! The metro pass, the cinema tickets, the university books, the espresso coffees. Everything has become more expensive! Now she understands why she has been running out of money so frequently! She suddenly feels ashamed for having suspected her little brother Pablo of taking her money to buy ice cream. "Che," she reassures herself, "Pablito would never do that."

After some hesitation, Josefina decides to approach her dad, Don Amancio, while he is in the kitchen sipping on his morning coffee. "Dad," Josefina calls timidly, "the stipend that you give me is no longer enough to take me through the month."

Amancio chokes on his drink. He coughs several times to clear his throat and finally raises his head to look at his daughter in disbelief. "*Cariño* (darling)," he says trying to remain calm, "what are you trying to tell me? That 2,000 pesos a month is not enough for you?" He then pauses, and his face becomes serious. "I am a father to eight children," he adds. "On the first day of every month, I give each and every one of my children 2,000 pesos. That is a lot of pesos, do you understand?"

Josefina nods quietly. She worries that Dad will become furious. "If all my children came to ask me for more money, I will be broke in no time," Amancio warns her. "So don't come and tell me that your stipend is not enough. You must be spending it irresponsibly, like most people of your age do!"

Josefina suddenly feels upset at this accusation. She searches for her little notebook and shows it to her dad. "Look, Dad," she says defiantly, "I am not lying. My spending habits have not changed, but I can no longer afford the same things. Prices are going up rapidly!"

Amancio flips through his daughter's notebook with his eyes wide open. He cannot believe that Josefina has gone through the pain of keeping a detailed diary of prices month after month. "*Hija mía* (my daughter)," Amancio says lowering his voice so that no one else can hear him, "I always knew that you were the shrewdest of my eight children. You have taken after your mother! You are right, prices are going up rapidly, and it is called *inflation*. When prices rise fast, every peso can buy fewer goods. This means that your affordability is being eroded by the day. You are right, your monthly stipend can no longer buy you the same things it was buying a year ago. For this reason, I will give you a 10 percent raise."

Josefina looks at her dad in a mischievous way. "But Dad," she adds, "my diary shows that prices have gone up by 30 percent. So if you only give me a 10 percent raise, it will still not be enough to afford me the same things I was buying before. For me to retain the same level of affordability, my stipend needs to increase in line with the increase in prices, that is, by 30 percent."

Amancio suddenly looks defeated. He puts his hand in his pocket and takes out some pesos from his wallet. "*Hijita* (little daughter)," he says, "take this money, and go away. But please do not tell your siblings about this."

Later that day, Amancio walks into his boss's office and asks for a salary increase "in line with inflation." He stresses these last words as he remembers the conversation he had with his daughter in the morning. Don Leonardo, Amancio's boss, accepts hesitantly. "I am only doing this because you are our company's top salesman, and we cannot afford to lose you," he says. "But I beg you not to tell any of your colleagues about this."

After work, Don Amancio rushes to the bank where he keeps his savings. "*Señorita* (miss)," he tells the cashier politely, "please withdraw all the savings from my account, and hand me the cash at your earliest convenience. I want to buy a car tomorrow and use the rest of my cash to stockpile some basic goods at home," Don Amancio explains. "Prices are escalating rapidly, and my pesos may soon be worth nothing! If I don't buy those items now, I won't be able to buy them in a few months' time. My cash sitting in the bank is losing value by the day: prices are going up by 30 percent a year while I am only getting a 5 percent savings rate from the bank. So I better hurry and buy some real assets to preserve my wealth before it vanishes!"

The cashier hands Amancio the money in several large envelopes that she places carefully in a plastic bag. Don Amancio thanks her profusely. "I have got eight children, *señorita*," he adds before leaving. "And they are getting shrewder by the day."

Key Concepts:

- Inflation refers to the general increase in the price of goods and services in an economy over a period of time. When there is high inflation (prices rise sharply), goods become more expensive, and the affordability of households and businesses gets eroded. This means that the same amount of money or income can buy fewer goods.

- Inflation is measured by comparing the price of a broad basket of goods over a given period of time.

- Sustained periods of high price increases (high inflation) are usually caused by the government printing too much money. The government of every country has exclusive control over the supply of money in an economy. This gives governments the ability to print money at their discretion.

- The responsible way for governments to finance their expenditure is by collecting tax revenue and borrowing prudently. However, because governments have exclusive control over the supply of money in a country, they can sometimes resort to printing large amounts of currency in order to finance their expenditure.

- When governments print too much money, the value of money gets eroded, and each unit of currency is worth less. This means that more units of currency are needed to buy the same products, driving prices up. As prices rise, affordability levels fall.

- High inflation is an indirect form of tax by the government because it takes away affordability (purchasing power) from people's incomes.

- There is a strong link between inflation and interest rates. In periods of high inflation, because affordability levels are falling, people are able to save less, and interest rates (the cost of borrowing) rise for all borrowers.

11. FOREIGN EXCHANGE: THE KENYAN MARKETING DIRECTOR

Muathi Kilonzo is a thirty-two-year-old marketing director at Kenyacom, one of Kenya's leading telecom operators. Muathi lives in an affluent neighborhood in Nairobi and earns 150,000 shillings a month (the equivalent of 1,500 US dollars). That is a lot of shillings for Muathi, who grew up in rural Kenya and is comfortable living on a fraction of that amount.

Muathi grew up in Makindu, a small town in south-eastern Kenya, where his parents still live. As a child, Muathi raised goats and chickens and helped his family farm maize and beans. Muathi also attended primary school in his hometown. However, in his distant recollections, he cannot remember sitting down in class in front of a teacher. Instead, more entertaining memories come to his mind—the times when he used to run around the bush with his friends trying to catch crickets and snails while they were supposed to be learning! And then of course, there was Mr. Mutunga, the instructor, who was often absent on sick leave and only showed up to class to give surprise exams.

It was only when he turned eleven that Muathi actually started learning something at school. Prosper, Muathi's paternal uncle and the most educated man in the family, soon realized that his nephew was falling behind academically. So he decided to send him to a better school in Nairobi, several hours away by bus.

"You will be a boarding student at a Presbyterian Boys' School," Uncle Prosper told Muathi. "You will finally learn how to behave like a Christian gentleman. Enough with the catching of crickets and snails during school hours!" he exclaimed, implying there was something inherently incompatible between the art of catching insects and that of being a gentleman.

"Never forget our traditional way of life," Muathi's father told his son before he left Makindu. "You can become as much of a gentleman as Uncle Prosper wants you to, but you should always remember to eat plentifully. My son," Father had continued, "I don't want you to disgrace our family by becoming one of those city people who work so hard that they become thin. A man's wealth shows in his stomach. So study hard, but also eat bountifully so that you may grow up to become rich and fat."

Muathi was a good son, and as such he honored his father's wishes. He grew up to become a *traditionally built* young man, that is, having very round cheeks and a prominent belly. He also excelled academically at the Presbyterian Boys' School and quickly learned how to behave like a Christian gentleman, leaving behind the childish habit of catching crickets.

Years later, Muathi continued to make his family proud. He started working as an intern at Kenyacom and rapidly got promoted to marketing director. And then he did what every successful man from his hometown would have done: he got married to his beloved. Muathi was elated. He had been able to attract the most beautiful girl from Makindu, Precious Mwenda.

Precious was also *traditionally built*, something that Muathi felt united them in a very special way, a bond much deeper than love or friendship. Shortly after their marriage, Precious moved to Nairobi with Muathi and soon became a very fashionable lady. "Beware of villagers," Uncle Prosper warned his nephew. "They are not used to having so much cash, and they will blow it away at the slightest opportunity." So Muathi put his wife Precious on a monthly stipend. As long as she did not ask for more, he was happy for her to do whatever she pleased with the money.

Precious loved walking around supermarkets and soon developed a taste for imported goods, such as French yogurts, Swiss cheese, and Italian wine. As for Muathi, outside of eating, his main hobbies were cars and technological gadgets. He purchased a Mercedes-Benz the moment he got promoted to marketing director, and he regularly visited the shopping mall to buy the latest video games and tech gadgets.

One day, Muathi gets to work and is asked to meet Mr. Polycarp Wekesa, Kenyacom's chief executive officer, in his office. As he enters the room, Muathi holds his breath and says a silent prayer. Suddenly, he feels sweat drops rolling down his chubby cheeks. Mr. Wekesa notices that Muathi is feeling uncomfortable and proceeds to say in a paternalistic way, "Take a seat, my son. Don't be worried. I have good news for you. You have worked very hard this year, and I am going to increase your salary by 10 percent."

"Thank you, sir," Muathi replies, relieved to hear the news. "I am personally indebted to you and will continue to work hard for this company. In the meantime, I remain at your disposal for any assistance you may require." And after saying these words, which he deemed to be worthy of a Christian gentleman, Muathi excused himself and walked out of the room.

The following weekend, Muathi drives to the shopping mall to buy a new smartphone and a touchscreen computer. "Technology is evolving fast," he tells himself, "and I must not fall behind." He picks up the gadgets and walks to the cashier. "It is 100,000 shillings (equivalent of 1,000 US dollars), sir," the cashier says politely.

Muathi feels instantly embarrassed. "100,000 shillings?" he repeats timidly. "But the price has gone up so much since I last checked."

"I am sorry, sir," replies the cashier, "that is the way things are."

Muathi checks his wallet and realizes that he does not have enough money to pay for the goods. "I shall come back another day," he says and drives back home in his Mercedes-Benz.

On his way home, Muathi thinks about what happened at the shopping mall. He wonders why the price of the gadgets he wanted to buy has gone up so much, exactly 30 percent, since he last checked. He compares the 30 percent price rise with his 10 percent salary increase, and all of a sudden, he realizes that he may still not be able to afford the new phone and computer. When he gets home, Muathi opens a newspaper and finds an interesting article about the depreciation of the shilling and the impact it is having on people's affordability:

Our country relies heavily on imported goods, such as computers, mobile phones, and other manufactured goods and industrial components. These imported goods are often priced in US dollars. When our currency, the shilling, loses value against the US dollar—also called *depreciation*—imported goods suddenly become more expensive to the average Kenyan. Over the last year, the shilling has lost about 30 percent of its value relative to the US dollar. This means that the same mobile phone, washing machine, or microwave now costs about 30 percent more shillings than a year ago, even though the price in US dollars has not changed. In practice, the depreciation of the shilling means that our people are getting poorer, as they can afford to buy fewer goods from abroad.

Muathi takes his time to digest what he is reading. He wishes he had paid more attention in economics class at university. But instead, he was writing love letters to Precious Mwenda and reminiscing about his school days back in Makindu, when he used to catch crickets and snails. But the article's message is loud and clear: the shilling has lost value relative to the US dollar, and that is why the smartphone and computer he wanted to buy have gotten more expensive.

A thought suddenly crosses Muathi's mind. He walks up to the kitchen and finds Precious savoring some Swiss cheese over a glass of Italian wine. "Enough with this!" Muathi says slightly annoyed. "Enough with cheese, yogurts, and wine! Uncle Prosper was right: you have become too fashionable! We are going back to the traditional way of life. From now on, we will be eating *ugali* (traditional cornmeal staple) and spinach stew every evening."

"That's fine," Precious replies calmly, "I can do with that. But you have to promise me that you will stop playing video games and that we will spend more time together."

Muathi laughs at Precious's suggestion and hugs her round body. "I will," he says, "but not because you say so, simply because I cannot afford to be buying the latest video games with the same frequency as before. The shilling has devalued, and imported goods are becoming too expensive."

"Don't worry about imported goods," Precious replies. "As long as we can afford to eat *ugali* and stew in large quantities, we will always be rich and fat. Isn't that the whole point of life?" she asks. Muathi cannot help but laugh, shaking his prominent belly up and down. Precious is right: a man's true wealth is in his stomach.

Key Concepts:

- In the same way that a country's national currency facilitates economic transactions within its borders, currencies such as the US dollar and the euro are widely used to facilitate international trade.

- Exchange rates represent the value of one currency in relation to another.

- A country's ability to consume foreign products depends on its foreign-currency earnings. Foreign-currency earnings are primarily derived from exporting goods to other countries, which are paid for in foreign currencies, such as US dollars or euros.

- When the value of a country's exports rises sharply, the value of its currency tends to appreciate (relative to other international currencies) because of stronger foreign-currency earnings.

- On the other hand, when a country's appetite for imported goods exceeds its foreign-currency earnings, the value of the national currency tends to depreciate. When a country's currency depreciates, imported goods become more expensive to local residents.

12. JOB CREATION: THE GREEK NEWS PRESENTER

Evangelos Assimakos is a high-profile TV presenter at Hellenic Broadcasting Corporation, the largest TV station in Greece. Evangelos has worked for Hellenic TV for the past twelve years and is a well-known face across the country. He reads the news every day at lunch time and is easily recognized by his radiant smile, his shiny black hair, and his elegant intonation.

Every time Evangelos goes for a walk around Ermou Street, one of Athen's busiest shopping alleys, people stop to greet him respectfully. "*Kalimera* (good morning), Mr. Assimakos, it is a pleasure to meet you."

Evangelos lives in a penthouse overlooking the Acropolis, together with his wife Dzifa, and their two sons, Aristotle and Socrates. When the boys are on summer holidays, the family takes a ferry to nearby Crete, where they spend weeks going to the beach and enjoying long walks on the Mediterranean mountains.

Aristotle and Socrates love mountain hiking and playing *explorers* in the bush. The two children pretend they are looking for hidden treasures in a faraway island and fill their pockets with all sorts of items they find in the mountains: funny-shaped stones, snail shells, cigarette stubs, and empty Coca-Cola cans that people have abandoned after their picnics.

It goes without saying that the Assimakos family is a happy one. They live a comfortable life, and even though Dzifa is a stay-at-home mom, Evangelos' salary is more than sufficient to afford the family little luxuries, such as those long holidays in Crete.

One day, Evangelos returns home from work looking defeated. Dzifa rushes up to him and asks him what has happened. "Have you been robbed on your way back home? Have you had an argument with your boss?"

"No, no," Evangelos says, "what has happened is far worse than that! Hellenic Broadcasting Corporation has gone bankrupt! As you know, the company was funded by the government, but because of the economic crisis, public spending has come under pressure, and the government can no longer afford to run the TV station. So the company is shutting down, and I have lost my job!" Evangelos laments.

"That is a real Greek tragedy!" Dzifa replies. "What will we do now?"

Evangelos spends the following weeks at home thinking about his future. For the last twelve years, he has been reading the news every day. It has become part of his lifestyle and his identity. It is all that he knows how to do, and now he feels lost. "My fate is a sad one," Evangelos tells himself. "Sadder than the fate of Prometheus," he concludes, referring to an ancient Greek play that he recently read.

"I had a stellar career ahead of me," Evangelos ponders. "I was about to be promoted to executive director. Everybody in Athens recognized my face and greeted me warmly. What will I become now? I dread the day when people just walk past me on Ermou Street without even muttering *kalimera*!" he says.

As weeks go by, Evangelos' mood becomes increasingly bitter. He feels gloomy without a job. In fact, so many Greek people are feeling gloomy. The country is undergoing a prolonged economic crisis, and unemployment is rising fast. Household incomes are going down, and nobody knows what to hold on to. The government owes too much money, and it has to make major cuts to public spending that are impacting people's daily lives. "Our government has failed us," discontented people protest in the streets of Athens and Thessalonica.

As time goes by, Dzifa suspects that Evangelos is getting depressed. He no longer spends hours every morning in front of the mirror combing his shiny black hair, and he does not tuck in his shirt before he goes for walks on Ermou Street. His physical appearance is deteriorating. His olive skin is losing its radiance, and his hair is turning gray.

"I have got something for you," Dzifa tells Evangelos one day. "I got you a ticket to go to Crete. It may be good for you to spend some time on your own and think about your future. The sight of the sea and the mountain breeze will appease your troubled soul. Go and come back. The children and I will be waiting for you."

Evangelos packs his bag and prepares to sail off to Crete. But before he leaves, he phones his mother, Elena, urging her to come over to keep Dzifa and the kids company while he is away.

"Aristotle and Socrates love your *moussaka* (traditional Greek dish), Mom, and you know that Dzifa's cooking is nowhere as good as yours," he adds, knowing that this little comment would make Mom proud.

When he reaches Crete, Evangelos decides to go for a long walk on the bushy mountains. How soothing the sight of the pristine Mediterranean Sea in the horizon! How peaceful the sound of the crickets in the mountain! How cool the breeze and how quiet without Aristotle and Socrates running around everywhere!

Evangelos pauses to admire the breathtaking views that stretch before his eyes. Far away, he can see the marina, the millionaires' yachts, the tourist ferries, and to the right, the laborious fishermen relentlessly throwing their nets into the calm sea. Around him, there are only a few scattered pine trees and a blanket of aromatic plants—lavender, rosemary, and thyme. He feels nature is embracing him in a warm hug, just like the hugs of his loving wife, Dzifa. "This is the most beautiful place in the world," Evangelos tells himself proudly. "No wonder that the greatest philosophers of mankind were born on this land and that amid these blue skies, the gods chose to make their abode."

Engulfed in these poetic thoughts and wandering around aimlessly, Evangelos suddenly bumps into something hard—a piece of wood. He looks down and realizes that he has stepped on a wooden sign. He flips it over and reads: Own a piece of heaven. Plot of land for sale here.

Evangelos writes down the phone number on the sign and starts walking back to town. As he descends the mountain, a brilliant idea crosses his mind. "This is divine inspiration," he tells himself. "In this godly land, ideas are bountiful."

What if he bought a plot of land in that mountain and set up a bed-and-breakfast hotel overlooking the sea? Dzifa would take care of the administration. He would do all the marketing and repairs. And as for Aristotle and Socrates, they could look after the ponies and play *explorers* every afternoon after school. This would be a fantastic way to create himself a job and to provide employment opportunities for other people, as he would need to hire cooks, gardeners, cleaners, and tourist guides.

Evangelos returns home after a week in Crete. "You are looking radiant again," Dzifa remarks proudly. "Your hair is well combed, and your shirt is tucked in. Your olive skin is glowing and…" Dzifa pauses. "Have you dyed your hair, sweetheart?"

"That is irrelevant, Dzifa," Evangelos retorts. "The most important thing that came out of my journey to Crete is that I have purchased a large plot of land in the mountain. We are going to set up a bed-and-breakfast hotel and create many jobs in the region!"

"Ah!" exclaims Dzifa in disbelief, "please tell me that this is a Greek comedy!"

Key Concepts:

- The availability of jobs in a country plays an important role in driving economic prosperity and social mobility. Employment provides individuals with a regular income and the opportunity to acquire new skills that can enrich their lives. But how are jobs created?

- When individuals set up businesses to produce goods or deliver services, they create jobs in the process. Governments also create employment opportunities in the process of providing public infrastructure and social services.

- As individuals, businesses, and governments identify more opportunities to create new products or services, more jobs are created. Societies that promote innovation and entrepreneurial activities tend to have higher levels of job creation.

13. THE ROLE OF GOVERNMENT IN THE ECONOMY: THE CONGOLESE MAYOR

Marcel Lokomba is an economics PhD who works for the World Bank in Washington, DC. After fourteen years in the job, Marcel decides to return to his hometown, Bukavu, in the Democratic Republic of Congo.

Marcel's life has been full of unexpected twists and turns. "My life," he ponders, "is like one of those popular Nigerian movies." When he looks back, Marcel realizes that he has spent most of his life chasing something.

As a child, Marcel chased pigs and cows on his grandfather's farm in Bukavu. When he grew a little older, he chased fish with his friends in Lake Kivu, where he learned how to swim. Soon afterward, Marcel chased the Belgian priest who was to sponsor him to attend seminary school in the region. When he completed seminary school, Marcel chased his grandfather, pleading with him to sell some of his farmland in order to pay for his university education in Kinshasa, over a thousand kilometers away from Bukavu. At the University of Kinshasa, Marcel studied mathematics, but he also ran around the campus chasing away stray dogs or rather being chased away by stray dogs, which he was very scared of.

This arduous task completed, Marcel chased the dean of the university, who was to write him a recommendation letter to pursue a master's degree in Geneva, Switzerland. In that foreign land, Marcel chased buses and trains like he had never done before. He completed his master's degree and got accepted into a PhD program at a reputable US university. But before he could travel to the United States, Marcel had to chase the American embassy to issue him a student visa. It all worked out in the end. He studied hard and completed his PhD, and one last time, Marcel chased and finally landed what was to be his job at the World Bank for the following fourteen years.

"I have done enough chasing in my life," Marcel tells himself. "It is now time for me to return to my homeland, the land of my ancestors, and serve my people. I will run for mayor of Bukavu!"

Marcel flies back to Bukavu where his wife, Beatrice, is waiting for him, with a succulent goat stew that she has prepared especially for him. While they are dining, Marcel tells Beatrice about his political ambitions.

"What would the name of your party be?" Beatrice asks.

"The Party for Bukavu's Youth," Marcel replies.

"Youth!" Beatrice repeats in a funny tone. "But look at yourself, Marcel, you are no longer a child!"

"Beatrice," Marcel says patiently, "the majority of people in Bukavu are under the age of twenty-five. That is why I have chosen that name for my party. It will resonate well with young voters. And besides, I am not that old. I was born on the year that the earth shook and the land around Lake Kivu flooded."

"That was a long time ago!" Beatrice insists.

"Anyway," interrupts Marcel, "you just need to look around." "I am much younger than the leader of the opposition party," Marcel concludes before going back to eating his goat stew.

Weeks later, Marcel and his wife move into a luxurious mountain villa overlooking Lake Kivu. While he is standing on the porch admiring the breathtaking views, Marcel thinks of the days when he used to chase pigs on his grandfather's farm. "He would be proud of me, my grandfather," Marcel tells himself. "This residence is worthy of a mayor!" he adds.

Over the following weeks, Marcel starts campaigning. He presents his electoral program at rallies, radio and TV stations. "Jobs, jobs, and more jobs," Marcel says. "My government will create jobs for the people, hiring more teachers, nurses, and policemen. We will also invest in infrastructure. The potholes on the road to Goma will get filled. The gutters on our streets will get covered. We will supply electricity and water to every home. We will renovate our primary schools and refurbish the general hospital, providing all the modern medical equipment that our people deserve! We will also introduce welfare payments for widows and orphans, to alleviate those who are struggling. Vote for me. Vote for your future!"

After several months, the big day arrives. Elections are held, and the Party for Bukavu's Youth wins by a large majority. Dr. Lokomba becomes the mayor of Bukavu!

"Let's get started," Marcel tells his assistant, Didier. "Please read all these documents, and prepare me a summary report on the state of our region's finances. Before our government starts spending money, we need to have a budget and see what we can afford."

A few days later, Didier approaches Marcel. "*Monsieur* (sir)," he says politely, "I have completed the report."

"Please read it aloud," Marcel orders, using the same intonation that those Belgian priests used to tell students what to do back in the days in seminary school. Didier proceeds:

"Most people in Bukavu are engaged in subsistence agriculture and informal trading. As a result, it is difficult to estimate their actual earnings and even more difficult to collect taxes from them. Regarding businesses in our region, the majority are *mom-and-pop* shops by the roadside that do not keep any accounts. It is hard to estimate how profitable these shops are and almost impossible to collect any tax from them.

There is, however, a large German pharmaceutical company in Bukavu that employs over a thousand people and is working on finding a cure for malaria. That company accounts for a large portion of the taxes that our government collects. The rest of our tax receipts come from Bukavu Savings Bank and Bukavu Telecom, the other large formal employers in the region.

As for how our budget is currently being spent, the vast majority of our revenue is used to paying for the wages of public-sector employees, including teachers, doctors, nurses, policemen, and public administrators. In fact, after paying for public-sector wages, we are left with very little money for maintaining schools and hospitals, fixing roads, and paving streets. Hence the dire state of our infrastructure.

Years ago the previous mayor took a big loan in order to build a hydraulic power station in Lake Kivu. His intention was good: he believed that better access to electricity will make it easier for businesses to thrive, creating jobs in the region and improving living standards. However, it soon became obvious that the loan was unaffordable and the district of Bukavu could no longer pay for it. In fact, our government is on the verge of bankruptcy. Our spending is much larger than the income we generate from tax collections. We have no money to continue paying public-sector wages and even less to invest in infrastructure," Didier concludes.

Marcel suddenly realizes the full scope of the task ahead of him. He takes Didier's report and hides in his office with several bottles of *Coca Cola*, his favorite drink. Weeks later, he appears at a press conference: "My people," Marcel says, "when I returned from abroad, I had a dream. I dreamed of transforming Bukavu into little Geneva. But our government's financial situation has turned out to be much weaker than I expected. Our budget is tight. We will have to make compromises and prioritize our spending. But with your support, we will make progress and continue walking toward the dream."

A few years later, Marcel's policies turn out to be a success. The government of Bukavu is able to repay its debt and starts keeping a tight eye on spending. By planning wisely and prioritizing, the government is able to invest in areas that benefit many people. The general hospital gets refurbished; the street gutters get covered; and as for the potholes on the road to Goma, well, there are still some potholes around, but a group of youth volunteers has taken it upon themselves to fill them with sand and mortar in their spare time.

There is still a lot of work to do, but Bukavu is slowly transforming itself into a better place. "The land of my ancestors is looking more and more like Geneva!" Marcel wonders proudly as he admires the scenic views from his villa. "No, actually," he pauses. "Nothing in the world compares to the beauty of the lakes and the mountains of Bukavu!"

Key Concepts:

- Governments play an important role in the economy. They provide critical public infrastructure and services, such as roads, schools, hospitals, a judiciary system, and national security.

- In order to pay for these services, governments rely on tax revenue. Tax revenue is derived from taxes on income, properties, and goods and services, as well as taxes on business profits.

- The level and sustainability of a government's spending depends on the amount of tax revenue it is able to generate every year. The extent to which a government can provide public infrastructure and social services depends on the size of its revenue.

- Since the primary source of government revenue comes from taxes, government spending is affected by the economic prospects of households and businesses. Government revenue grows faster in periods of stronger economic growth.

- When government expenditure exceeds its revenues, governments can borrow money to fund the gap. But governments must spend and borrow prudently in order to support economic growth and stability.

- When governments rely excessively on borrowing to finance large spending plans, this often leads to economic instability. Excessive government borrowing often leads to high interest rates and makes it more costly for households and businesses to borrow money for investments.

14. RISK AND RETURN: THE ITALIAN ANTHROPOLOGIST

Giorgio Ramazzotti is a thirty-seven-year-old anthropologist who lives in Vinci, a picturesque village in the Italian Tuscany. Giorgio lives in a rural cottage overlooking an olive orchard, with his wife, Teresa, and their two children, Alma and Romeo.

Giorgio grew up in a comfortable home in Rome. His father, Don Enrico, was the owner of a ceramic-tile business, while his mother, Donna Maddalena, was a homemaker. Giorgio had every luxury a child could enjoy while he was growing up, but he always felt constrained by the four walls of his family's apartment. He dreamed of the day when he could live closer to nature.

Giorgio studied anthropology at the University of Rome, and as soon as he graduated, he moved to Vinci, the most remote village he could find in the mountains of Tuscany, far away from Don Enrico and Donna Maddalena. Over there, he moved into an old cottage that he refurbished and made his home.

Don Enrico and Donna Maddalena became very upset at their son's decision to move to the countryside and lead a bohemian lifestyle. "*Cavalieri* (gentlemen) don't have long hair like you do, Giorgio," Donna Maddalena lamented. But Don Enrico was cruder about his views: "Earrings are for girls," he told his son dismissively. But nothing that Don Enrico and Donna Maddalena could say made Giorgio change his lifestyle, and his parents soon gave up on him.

Years later, Giorgio met Teresa, a beautiful pharmacist-turned-herbalist who instantly felt attracted to everything that Don Enrico and Donna Maddalena disliked about their son.

Teresa and Giorgio got engaged, moved together, and had children in the land of Tuscany. During their engagement ceremony, Giorgio gifted Teresa two cows and ten chickens, the latter of which were to have many chicks. Teresa gladly accepted these gifts as a bohemian promise of eternal love.

Soon afterward, Giorgio's career started to pick up. Some of the articles that he wrote in the tranquility of his Tuscan cottage got published in reputable anthropology journals, and he soon started receiving invitations to speak at conferences in Florence and Milan. A few months later, Giorgio got invited to host a TV series on the Italian History Channel. His professional success, coupled with his frugal lifestyle, soon resulted in Giorgio making a good amount of savings.

"Money burns people's hands," Don Enrico warned Giorgio when he was just a child. "You must either use money, or money will end up using you," he added. And because Giorgio was slightly superstitious, he decided to follow his father's advice and take the best of the two choices he was presented with: using his money.

The following day, Giorgio walked into Vinci Savings Bank. He picked up a glossy brochure entitled "Savings" and showed it to his wife, Teresa, later that day. Giorgio had been raised under the strict orders of Donna Maddalena, his *Mamma*, and in the absence of this matriarchal figure, Teresa was to become the key decision-maker in his household.

After reading the brochure, Teresa told Giorgio, "The bank offers you a number of saving plans. The interest rate the bank pays for your savings depends on how long you are willing to lock your money away for. For instance, if you choose to lock your money away in a one-year deposit, the bank will pay you 2 percent interest rate per year on your savings. If you opt for a two-year deposit, you will get 3 percent interest. This makes sense: the longer you are willing to lock your savings away for, the higher the return the bank has to offer you in order to compensate you for not having access to your money."

"Those interest rates are low!" Giorgio complained, "so low that I do not want to lock my money away in exchange for such little compensation! I'd rather do something else with my cash!"

One day, Giorgio receives a phone call from his cousin, Benedetto, who lives in Palermo, the capital city of Sicily. Benedetto dropped out of school at the age of sixteen and had since had a variety of occupations. He worked as a mason building houses, then as a chef baking pizza, and finally as a bus driver taking tourists around. But Benedetto's dream had always been to set up a business so that he would never again have a boss to report to.

"*Ciao* (hello), Giorgio," Benedetto says over the phone, "I need to ask you for a big favor. You know that the situation is very rough here in Sicily. Banks won't lend me any money, but I have a fantastic business opportunity that could turn both of us into millionaires!"

Benedetto explains that he wants to set up a horse-riding school on the outskirts of Palermo. "Tourists would love to explore this region on horseback," he adds. Then he explains that he has managed to save enough money to lease several hectares of land and build the wooden stables where the horses would live. "But I need some help buying twenty pure-bred Arab horses," Benedetto says. "Those beasts are expensive, you know!" he adds.

Benedetto feels that Giorgio is hesitant over the phone and continues, "We are cousins, aren't we, Giorgio? You are *blood of my blood*! If you lend me some money, I will pay you an 8 percent interest annually in exchange for your generosity." Giorgio suddenly feels inclined to lend Benedetto some money and tells him that he will think about the proposal.

"Beware of your cousin Benedetto," Donna Maddalena warns Giorgio. "I once lent him money to set up a *gelateria* (ice-cream shop) in Palermo, and I never got a cent back!" she adds.

But Giorgio cannot help but think about the 8 percent interest that his cousin is offering him. It sounds so much more appealing than what the bank is offering him for his savings. "I will ask Teresa for her opinion," Giorgio concludes.

That evening, Teresa listens to Giorgio's story as she enjoys a warm *lasagna* (traditional Italian dish) over supper. Outside, Romeo and Alma are climbing olive trees and catching butterflies.

"*Mio caro* (my darling)," Teresa says, "the 8 percent interest that your cousin Benedetto is offering you in exchange for lending him money is not a bargain," she says. "In fact, it makes sense that he offers you a much greater return than the bank does. The higher the risk of losing money, the greater the reward you need to compensate you for taking the extra risk." Then she continues, "Investing in Benedetto's business venture is far riskier than locking your money in the bank. You can be pretty sure that the bank will keep your money safe and pay you interest in a timely manner. However, when it comes to Benedetto's horse-riding school, who knows what will happen? Will the school make enough profits to repay the loan? What if the number of tourists who want to horse ride is not as large as anticipated? What if some of the Arab horses get injured? And what if Benedetto simply decides to run away with your money?"

"Benedetto would never do that!" Giorgio responds firmly. "He is my cousin, the *blood of my blood*!"

"So what happened to that *gelateria* that he wanted to set up?" Teresa asks inquisitively.

Giorgio blushes, as he usually does when his *Mamma*, Donna Maddalena, catches him in a difficult situation. "Teresa, we all make mistakes in our youth," he concludes.

Outside, Romeo and Alma continue chasing butterflies as the sun sets over the picturesque Tuscany.

Key Concepts:

- Banks make money by taking deposits from savers and using those funds to provide loans to borrowers. The difference between the interest rate that banks charge on loans and what they pay to savers on deposits represents the core income of a bank.

- Savers are only willing to deposit money in a bank when they trust that their money will be safe. As a result, banks have to be prudent about who they lend to.

- Banks charge higher interest rates on loans made to riskier borrowers to compensate for the additional risks associated with the repayment of the loan.

- Because a bank's business is reliant on deposits from savers, banks will typically not lend at all when they estimate a borrower's risk of repayment to be too high.

15. SAVINGS AND INVESTMENTS: THE SRI LANKAN NURSERY OWNER

Chandrika Udawatta is a twenty-four-year-old technology graduate from Kandy, Sri Lanka's second largest city. Chandrika lives in a spacious colonial house in Kandy's city center, along with her aunt, Ruchira, and her father, Appa.

Chandrika studied information technology at the University of Colombo. Over there, she learned everything there was to be learned about writing software code and creating computer programs. However, as soon as she graduated, she realized that a career in technology was not for her. She had a different passion: working with children.

But Chandrika's family was unimpressed by her decision to pursue her true interests. "You have a bright future in front of you. Don't spoil it," Auntie Ruchira warned her. "Stick to technology. All the people you see driving around Kandy in big cars have made money from it," she pointed out. But Chandrika was not interested in her aunt's views. She had made up her mind.

One morning, Auntie Ruchira found Chandrika sweeping the courtyard diligently and polishing the floors. "You finally dare to take a broom and do some cleaning, young lady!" Auntie exclaimed. "Why are you working so hard?" she asked.

"Auntie," Chandrika said firmly, "I am going to use our courtyard to set up a crèche."

"A crèche!" Auntie exclaimed. "Of all the jobs in the world you could think of…And what are you planning to do with your technology diploma? Will you use it to change babies' nappies?" Auntie asked.

But Chandrika pretended she had not heard her auntie's comments. Everyone was entitled to their own opinions, and she was determined to achieve her goals. Over the following days, Chandrika painted the courtyard's walls in bright colors and arranged for a carpenter to build several wood shelters that would serve as classrooms. The following week, she went to the market and purchased some educational equipment, several toddler bicycles, and a few fancy toys.

A week later, Chandrika raised a large sign outside her house that read "Kandy's First Montessori Crèche: Now Open." Over the following weeks, families started pouring in to enroll their children. "I want my child to learn English from an early age," one mother said. "I want my child to play with those fancy toys I never had," a father added. Enrollment numbers kept growing, and a few months later, Kandy's First Montessori Crèche was full. The crèche had over sixty toddlers and ten ladies employed as carers.

"This crèche business was not such a bad idea, after all," Auntie Ruchira says. "Somehow people are attracted to the word *Montessori*," she continues. "It sounds fancy and foreign. Although I am not quite sure what it means."

"Me neither," Chandrika replies. "But I saw it written everywhere when I visited Uncle Roshan in Colombo last year. I told myself that if it works in Colombo, it must work in Kandy too."

One day, as Chandrika is playing with the toddlers, an idea crosses her mind. Her nursery is full, and she has to turn parents away. What if she opened a second Montessori crèche? She estimates that she may need about 730,000 rupees (the equivalent of 5,000 US dollars) to set up a second nursery. But where would she get that sort of money from? Her current business is making a profit and generating cash, but she would need to wait several years before she can save that amount of money. "Or perhaps not," Chandrika tells herself. She could go to the bank and ask for a loan.

"Beware of loans!" Appa warns her daughter when he hears about her plans. "When you were just a child," Appa continues, "your mother and I almost lost everything we had because of those evil loans. It was a long time ago, when you were just a baby and we lived in our native village of Menikdiwela. We were poor rice farmers. We had little knowledge and big dreams for the future. One morning, as your mother was grinding coconuts in the courtyard, a nice city gentleman stopped by our village. He was wearing a neatly pressed shirt and a tie. He was driving a motorbike. He said he worked for some lending institution, and he asked us if we needed money."

"'What sort of question is that?' I asked the gentleman in awe. 'Of course we need money! We are poor farmers from Menikdiwela village, not ministers!' I told him. The gentleman explained that he could lend us a large sum of money and we could pay it off overtime. He went on explaining many complicated things. *Interest rates, installments, percentages*...God knows what! Your mother and I could not care the least. We were just thinking of everything we would do with that money. We used our fingerprints to sign off some forms that we could not read, and finally, the friendly gentleman handed us a bag full of rupees! Your mother and I had never seen that many rupees together in our lifetime! It was the happiest moment of our lives," Appa said.

"The first thing we did was to cement our mud house," he continued. "That way we would never again have to fix the walls during the monsoon season, when the strong rains usually eroded them. We also bought a cow so that we could sell its milk. After doing this, we still had some money left, so we bought a color television. That made us very popular in the village! On weekends, we would plug the TV to a car battery and set it up in the courtyard. Then everyone would stop by to watch cricket. Those were happy days. But our joy did not last long."

"A few weeks later," Appa continued, "the gentleman with the neatly ironed shirt came over to ask for the first loan payment. The amount he quoted was so large that we had to give him all the cash we had on us. The following week, the gentleman came back asking for more. We did not have enough money, and he said that we should find a way to pay him or he would take away our television and our cow. 'Not our cow!' your mother and I shouted in unison, as this was our most precious asset.

It was then that your mother had an idea. 'What if we take another loan to pay off this one?' So we approached another man wearing a neatly pressed shirt and a tie, and we took another loan. It turned out to be the biggest mistake of our lives. Shortly afterward, there were not one but two city gentlemen chasing us for money! Every week the amount we owed them became larger and larger. It soon became clear that we could never pay back our loans.

One day, some very rude men working for the lending institution broke into our house. They took away everything we had: our cow, our television, our radio, our stove, our bicycle, and even your mother's jewelry! I felt heartbroken when I saw your mother's dowry go into the hands of those people! But the story was not over. Those men kept chasing us and taking every little money we managed to make for several years to come. Our life became really miserable, and we regretted the day we ever borrowed a single rupee! We should have been content with what we had, but our ambition led us astray! So I am telling you, my daughter, do not make the same mistake your mom and I made. Stay away from loans!"

"But Appa," Chandrika says patiently, "my situation is different from yours. You were poor farmers borrowing money for consumption at exorbitant interest rates, whereas I am a professional taking a loan to grow my business. I will only take the amount of debt that I can comfortably afford to repay with my business's cash flow. I will never put myself under that strain."

The following day, Chandrika dresses in her best *saree* (traditional Sri Lankan cloth) and walks into a bank carrying her nursery's financial results under her arm. She hands them to the bank manager and explains that she would like to take a loan in order to open a second nursery. The bank manager inspects the business's results and says, "Your business does have good prospects. We can lend you the amount you need at a 15 percent interest rate."

Chandrika goes home and thinks about the bank's proposal. She takes out her calculator and punches some numbers. "There is no way I can afford to pay such high interest on a loan," she tells herself. "The interest payments will suck away most of the cash my business generates, and it will take me very long to repay the loan. Appa was right," she ponders. "I should stay away from loans and be content with what I have."

A few years later, Chandrika manages to save enough money to open a second Montessori nursery in Kandy. The new nursery becomes an instant success, and the spaces fill up quickly. Business is thriving, and she is generating a growing amount of cash. "Perhaps now that my business is larger," Chandrika tells herself, "I can afford to take on a loan and open a third Montessori nursery!"

Chandrika walks into the bank and greets the bank manager who instantly recognizes her. "I can lend you the amount you need at a 6 percent interest rate," the bank manager tells her.

Chandrika is pleased to hear that the cost of borrowing has gotten cheaper. She punches some numbers in her calculator. "I will be glad to accept your loan, sir," she says. "My business is now larger than it was when I first asked for a loan. It now generates more cash, and the debt burden will not be as high this time around. I shall be able to pay off the debt in a couple of years."

And so it is that only a few years after graduating from university with a technology degree, Chandrika is the proud owner of three Montessori crèches in Kandy. She now employs over forty staff members and teaches plenty of children how to pronounce fancy English words.

"Your technology degree has turned out to be useful for changing babies' nappies," Auntie Ruchira says. "That Montessori idea of yours was not a bad one, after all."

Key Concepts:

- Households, businesses, and governments carry out investment activities. A family may invest in a new home, businesses may want to expand their production facilities, and governments may wish to invest in infrastructure. But how are investments funded?

- Investments are funded from current income and savings, but when this is not enough, investors rely on external sources of funds. Many large investments are funded by loans from banks and other financial institutions.

- Most of the funds available for lending in the economy come from savings. When there is a strong savings culture within households and businesses, and when the government spends within its means, there are more funds available for investments, and the cost of borrowing (interest rates) is likely to be low.

- Lower interest rates make it possible for individuals and businesses to fund a greater number of investment activities.

- Interest rates change overtime as savings habits and investment demand change. Interest rates are high (or rise) when investment demand is higher than the amount of savings available in the economy. Interest rates are low (or fall) when there is adequate savings relative to the level of investment demand.

16. FINANCIAL ACCOUNTING: THE IRANIAN APPRENTICE BAKER

Mohsen Ansari is a sixteen-year-old apprentice baker from Isfahan, a beautiful city in the heart of Iran. Mohsen works in his uncle's bakery and spends his days learning how to make *naan* bread (Iranian flatbread). Uncle Reza's bakery is one of the most successful in the bazaar. Every day, hundreds of men and women queue to buy their delicious bread. In the evenings, Uncle teaches Mohsen how to keep the bakery's accounts up-to-date.

"Keeping good accounts," Uncle Reza always tells his nephew, "is as important to the well-being of our bakery as making good bread. I know many shops in this bazaar that had plenty of customers but were forced to shut down because they were poorly managed."

"By keeping regular accounts and analyzing them frequently," Uncle Reza explains, "I am able to tell how efficiently my bakery is running. When I encounter problems, these accounts tell me where the problems are coming from. When I have to make decisions, these accounts help me take the right choices and avoid costly mistakes. These accounts help me plan the future wisely so that I can continue doing what I love…baking *naan* bread!"

Every evening, Uncle Reza seats down with his nephew Mohsen and shows him a large notebook where he keeps the bakery's accounts. "Since I don't have any sons," Uncle tells Mohsen, "one day you shall take over this business. So listen carefully to what I say. I will take you through our bakery's *Profit and Loss Account*. This is one of the most important financial statements that every business should produce."

Uncle Reza opens his large notebook carefully and starts talking to his nephew:

Sales: Our sales represent all the money that goes into our cashier every month. It can be calculated by multiplying the number of *naan* breads we sell by the price of each *naan*. Our sales go up when we sell more bread or when we increase the price of bread. But sales are seasonal. For example, during the month of *Ramadan* (the Muslim month of fasting), our sales usually halve because very few customers shop during the day. However, when *Ramadan* is over and comes the time to celebrate *Eid*, our sales usually triple as customers buy lots of bread to share large meals with family and friends.

Cost of Ingredients: This is the cost of producing the *naan* bread that we sell. It includes the cost of all the ingredients we use, such as flour, yeast, salt, and yogurt. Last year, wheat farmers had a poor harvest, and as a result, the cost of flour went up by 40 percent. We were forced to put prices up, and our customers complained a lot. But we explained to them that our ingredients had become more expensive and we had to increase prices in order to make the same amount of money we were making before.

Operating Expenses: Apart from the cost of ingredients, our business also incurs several running costs every month. We need to pay the wages of our employees, pay rent for the premises we use, and also buy firewood for the oven. Our expenses vary from month to month, and this has an impact on the amount of profits that our bakery makes. Last year during *Eid*, I gave all my employees some extra cash to take home. That meant our profits were lower that month, but it was worth it. You should see how happy the employees were!

Repayment of Loans: Some people take loans to grow their business or buy equipment, and they repay these loans overtime. The repayment of a loan reduces the cash a business makes. When the loan to be repaid is too large relative to the size of the business, it can sometimes get shops into trouble. But Uncle Reza never borrows money as a matter of principle, so this is not something we need to worry about.

Taxes: Every year, all the shops in the bazaar have to pay tax to the municipality of Isfahan. We pay a levy in exchange for the right to use the bazaar. The government then uses that money to keep the bazaar clean, provide lighting and security.

Net Profit: When we subtract all the bakery's expenses from the initial sales figure, we get the business's net profit. This represents the final profit that our bakery makes from selling bread, after deducting all the costs that occur from running the shop.

Mohsen looks satisfied with his uncle's explanations, but he seems to have some unanswered questions. "And after all this, Uncle, what do you do with your bakery's profits?" he asks curiously. "Do you keep all the money in your house, hidden somewhere?"

"No, Mohsen," Uncle Reza replies gently, "I usually divide my bakery's profits into three equal parts," he says. "One third of the profits always gets reinvested in the bakery. It is very important for businesses to retain a good level of cash in order to fund bulk purchases of ingredients, pay an advance on rent, and be able to cover any unexpected repairs," Uncle explains.

"I keep another third of the profits to provide for my family's needs, pay for my children's education, and afford a visit to the village once a year," Uncle adds.

"What about the rest of your profits, Uncle? What do you do with them?" Reza asks impatiently.

"As for the remaining third of my profits," Uncle says, "I use them for *zakat* (alms in Islamic tradition), to help those people that are in need, such as orphans and widows."

"That is very good indeed," Mohsen replies. "But when I grow up, I am afraid that I don't want to be a baker," he confesses. "Instead I would like to open my own souvenir shop in the bazaar. There are many tourists in Isfahan these days, and I would like to sell them things to take home," Mohsen says.

"That sounds like a good idea," Uncle Reza replies. "The good news is that most businesses operate in much the same way. So you will be able to apply all the principles you learn in this bakery to your own souvenir shop," he says. "But now let's go back to baking *naan* bread. There are more customers arriving."

Key Concepts:

- Keeping accurate and timely financial records is an integral part of running a business. The availability of reliable financial information facilitates business decision making.

- Financial accounts provide a transparent measure of how a business is performing. They provide an objective basis to assess business profitability, identify underperforming areas, and assist with planning for the future.

17. CIVIC VALUES: THE CUBAN SALSA DANCER

Yamil Flores is a twenty-six-year-old salsa dancer from Santiago de Cuba, a vibrant city in the eastern part of the island. Yamil lives with his seventy-three-year-old grandfather, Don Eliades, in a charming colonial house located in the heart of the city.

Yamil studied civil engineering at the University of Santiago, and upon graduation he got employed by a government-owned engineering company. However, he quit after only three months in the job, when his friend Ibrahim pointed out to him that he could make five times more money teaching tourists how to dance salsa.

Don Eliades, Yamil's grandfather, became very upset when he heard about his grandson's drastic career change. "*Carajo* (hell)!" Don Eliades complained, "I did not raise you to become a street dancer!" Yamil tried to reassure his grandfather.

"*Viejo* (old man)," he told him, "God has given every person a different talent. Singers live off their voices. Mechanics live off their hands. And other people, like myself, live off their bodies! There is no shame in that. We should be proud of our gifts." But Don Eliades never bought his grandson's arguments.

One day, Yamil returns home from dancing salsa and finds Don Eliades in his usual position: he is resting on a cane chair outside the front door, enjoying the afternoon breeze. "Come closer, young man," Don Eliades orders. "What are you hiding in your pocket? Is that a mobile phone?" he asks. "*Diablos* (hell)!" the old man exclaims, "where on earth did you get the money to buy that horrendous piece of technology?"

Yamil starts mumbling. "I found it on the beach, *Viejo*," he replies. "Some tourist must have dropped it," he adds.

"*Mentiroso* (liar)!" Eliades shouts at the same time that he uses one of his sandals to spank his grandson. "That phone does not belong to you! You must return it to its owner," he commands.

"But I am telling you that it does not have an owner," Yamil repeats.

Don Eliades' voice becomes severe: "Everything in life has an owner, Yamil. Just like the flowers belong to the mountain and the love of Juanita belongs to Chan Chan," he says referring to a newlywed couple that lived nearby. "In that same way, that mobile phone belongs to someone else, not yourself. You must return it."

"But *Viejo*," Yamil confesses, "I need this mobile phone. Walking around Santiago without a phone these days is like showing up in Parliament without wearing a *guayabera* (traditional linen shirt). It is a must-have."

"What do you know about must-haves?" the old man interrupts angrily. "Have you ever lacked any basic necessities in your life?" he asks. "Our government provides food and basic needs to all its citizens. The problem is that young people are ungrateful. You take everything for granted. You have no values! In fact, you would sell our nation for a pair of jeans if you could!"

"Do as I say," Don Eliades continues. "Return that phone to its owner. It is a matter of civic values." Yamil looks amused.

"Civic what?" he asks his grandfather.

"Civic values," Don Eliades replies. "When I was growing up in this country, children were taught to consider the impact of their actions on other people's lives, to act with solidarity, and to take initiative to build a better world. When I was twenty-one, for instance, I participated in a state-sponsored youth volunteering program that took university students, like myself, to the countryside. Over there, we taught peasants and their children how to read and write. Back then, we all believed in a better Cuba, where poverty and ignorance would forever be eradicated. Now tell me, my grandson, in your daily life, how often do you make conscious contributions to society?" Don Eliades asks.

"Ay *Viejo*," Yamil replies, "when it comes to civic actions, I must be one of the top scorers in the neighborhood. You can ask my friend Ibrahim. He even calls me *Madre Teresa* (Mother Teresa). Such is my generosity and my goodwill. The other day, for instance, I bumped into a tourist who had just landed in Santiago. She was standing in a bar trying to move to the rhythms of our music. But she was so clumsy that I felt pity for her. So I approached her and took control of the situation. By the end of the evening, she was dancing like a TV star! Isn't that an example of civic values, *Viejo*?"

"I have tolerated enough nonsense!" Don Eliades concludes, and he retires to his bedroom to take an afternoon *siesta* (nap).

Later that day, while Eliades is sitting in his balcony looking at passersby, he hears his grandson's voice. "There is someone I want you to meet, *Viejo*," Yamil shouts. Don Eliades anticipates that something exciting is about to happen. He quickly combs his hair and sprays some perfume. He then changes into his finest *guayabera* and wears an old-fashioned hat.

"Meet Celia," Yamil says while he points at a seventy-odd-year-old lady dressed in her best Sunday clothes. "She asked me for directions to the cathedral, and because she looked a bit tired, I invited her to our house to have some coffee. Now, tell me, is this not a contribution to society, *Viejo*?" Yamil asks.

But Don Eliades has no time for his grandson's jokes. His eyes are stuck to the newcomer. "*Mi señora* (my lady)," Don Eliades says courteously, "allow me to say that you look as charming as Omara Portuondo (popular Cuban singer) when she started singing in the fifties."

"I know that," the old lady says proudly. "You are not the first person who tells me." Don Eliades invites Celia to sit on a cane chair next to him and serves her some freshly brewed coffee. While the old lady is busy sipping on her drink, Don Eliades takes Yamil to one corner.

"My grandson," he says quietly, "what you have just done may not be a contribution to society, but it is certainly an act of generosity toward me!"

"I figured that you had been lonely for too long, *Viejo*!" Yamil says, before he leaves the room to let the old couple chat at their ease.

Key Concepts:

- Civic values can have a meaningful impact on living standards. By promoting harmony and order in society, civic values create an environment of cooperation and social stability.

- To promote the development of civic values, individuals need to consider the impact of their actions on other members of society. Opportunities for social cooperation (such as volunteering) can support the provision of valuable services to the community.

ABOUT THE AUTHOR

Elena Fernandez Prados was born in Spain where she attended the French School of Murcia. Elena holds a BA in Business Economics and International Relations from Brown University (USA). She started her career working as an investment banking financial analyst at Morgan Stanley in London, before becoming a portfolio manager and investment director at Standard Life Investments in Edinburgh. Elena currently works as a consultant and lives in London.

Printed in Great Britain
by Amazon